MW01007510

Simply Ming™
AIR FRYER
COOKBOOK

Simply Ming™

AIR FRYER
COOKBOOK

SIMPLE & HEALTHIER FRIED RECIPES

© 2017 Castle Point Publishing

All rights reserved. No portion of this book may be reproduced or transmitted in any form or by any means, electronic or mechanical, including photocopying, recording, and other information storage and retrieval systems, without prior written permission of the publisher.

Cover and interior design by Katie Jennings Campbell

Castle Point Publishing
58 Ninth Street Hoboken, NJ 07030
www.castlepointpub.com

ISBN: 978-0-9981043-1-7

Please note: Read the safety instructions that came with your air fryer before trying any of the recipes in this book. The author, publisher, manufacturer, nor distributor can assume responsibility for the effectiveness of the recipes or text herein and shall have no liability for damages (whether direct, indirect, consequential, or otherwise) arising from the use, attempted use, misuse, or application of the directions described in this book. Some recipes may contain raw eggs or other ingredients. Consuming raw or undercooked meats, poultry, seafood, shellfish, or eggs may increase your risk of foodborne illness, especially if you have certain medical conditions. Consume at your own risk.

Simply Ming and Ming Tsai are registered trademarks of Ming Tsai, Ming East-West, LLC

Printed and bound in the United States of America

10 9 8 7 6 5 4 3 2 1

CONTENTS

INTRODUCTION

If you love fried foods—or cooking delicious food, fast—you're going to love air frying! An air fryer works like a deep-fryer to make food that's crispy on the outside and tender, juicy, and flavorful on the inside. And it does it with a fraction of the fat!

But the air fryer can do so much more than just make fried classics like French fries, onion blossoms, and mozzarella sticks. It's also a quick and easy way to prepare beautiful buffalo wings, flank steak, garlic bread, fish fillets, and more. You can even dehydrate fruit in it, and make amazing desserts!

Inside this book, you'll find all these recipes and then some. I've given you a wide range of different kinds of dishes, so you can experiment on your own once you have these down. Don't be afraid to throw your favorite vegetables in the air fryer and let them roast! Or, use your own favorite meatball or pork chop recipes (for example), using the times and temperatures I've listed for you here. With the air fryer, the possibilities are endless. Enjoy!

—Ming Tsai

CHIPS, BREADS, AND SNACKS

Easy Air-Fried **KALE CHIPS**

KALE CHIPS ARE CRUNCHY, HEALTHY, AND DELICIOUS—and they couldn't be easier to make in the air fryer. Not only is using the air fryer easy, but it gives them the perfect crisp.

---

1 BUNCH KALE

1 TABLESPOON EXTRA-VIRGIN OLIVE OIL

1 TEASPOON KOSHER SALT

1. Tear kale leaves into large pieces. Wash and dry thoroughly.

2. Set the air fryer to 200ºF. Place kale pieces in the air fryer basket and cook until very crispy, about 10 minutes, tossing leaves halfway through the cook time.

3. Toss chips with olive oil and salt, and enjoy.

Five-Spice
POTATO CHIPS

IF YOU'VE NEVER HAD HOMEMADE POTATO CHIPS, prepare to fall in love! This version flavors them with Chinese Five Spice powder, but you can use any of your favorite spices (like garlic or chili powder)—or just use some plain sea salt.

2 MEDIUM POTATOES, THINLY SLICED (PEELED, IF DESIRED)

1 TEASPOON CHINESE FIVE-SPICE POWDER

1/2 TEASPOON KOSHER SALT

1. Blanch potato slices in boiling water for 1 to 2 minutes. Drain, spread on paper towels, and dry very well.

2. Set the air fryer to 325ºF. Working in batches, place potato slices in a single layer in the air fryer basket, and cook for 5 minutes. Flip, cook for 5 more minutes, check for crispness, and continue cooking in 2-minute increments until crispy. Repeat with remaining potato slices.

3. Sprinkle with five-spice powder and salt and serve.

Dehydrated BEET CHIPS

MANY PEOPLE DON'T REALIZE that air fryers can also be used as dehydrators! Dehydrated beets are a delicious and unique snack perfect for the fall and winter.

---

2 BEETS, PEELED

KOSHER SALT

1. Slice beets thinly, preferably on a mandolin. Spread on paper towels, and pat dry.

2. Set the air fryer to 300ºF. Place beet slices in a single layer in the air fryer basket, and cook for 10 minutes.

Flip, cook for 5 more minutes, and check for crispness. If needed, continue cooking in 5-minute increments until crispy.

3. Sprinkle with salt to taste and serve.

Dehydrated PINEAPPLE CHIPS

DEHYDRATED PINEAPPLE CHIPS ARE A PERFECT SNACK for satisfying your sweet tooth. Make a batch and take them with you for an on-the-go treat.

1 (20-OUNCE) CAN OF PINEAPPLE
RINGS, OR 1 FRESH PINEAPPLE,
PEELED, CORED, AND CUT INTO
1-INCH-THICK SLICES

1. Set the air fryer to 200ºF. Working in batches, place pineapple slices in a single layer in the air fryer basket, and cook for 20 minutes.

2. Turn slices over and cook until dry but still soft, about another 20 minutes. Repeat with remaining pineapple slices. Serve immediately or store in a sealed container.

Roasted CHICKPEAS

FULL OF PROTEIN (AND INEXPENSIVE, TOO!), roasted chickpeas are a tasty and nutritious snack that are great for after school or after work. And in the air fryer, they couldn't be easier!

1 (29-OUNCE) CAN CHICKPEAS, DRAINED AND PATTED DRY

1 TEASPOON EXTRA-VIRGIN OLIVE OIL

1 TABLESPOON GARLIC SALT

1 TABLESPOON CHOPPED FRESH ROSEMARY

1. Set the air fryer to 350°F.

2. In a medium bowl, toss the chickpeas with the olive oil and the garlic salt. Place chickpeas in the air fryer basket, and cook for 10–15 minutes. Toss, and cook until very crispy, about 5 more minutes.

3. Add rosemary before serving.

HOMEMADE PITA CHIPS
with Eggplant-Olive Tapenade

WHY BUY EXPENSIVE PITA CHIPS at the store, when you can make them quickly and easily at home in the air fryer? This recipe pairs them with a delicious eggplant-olive tapenade, made with eggplant roasted (where else?) in the air fryer.

1 SMALL EGGPLANT

4–5 PITAS

COOKING SPRAY

1 TABLESPOON MADRAS CURRY POWDER, TOASTED IN A DRY SAUTÉ PAN

3 TABLESPOONS EXTRA-VIRGIN OLIVE OIL

KOSHER SALT AND FRESHLY GROUND BLACK PEPPER

1 TEASPOON MINCED GARLIC

1 TABLESPOON HONEY

1 TABLESPOON CHINESE BLACK OR BALSAMIC VINEGAR

1 BUNCH SCALLIONS, THINLY SLICED

1/4 CUP MINCED NIÇOISE OLIVES

1. Cut eggplant in half lengthwise. Set the air fryer to 400ºF. Place eggplant in the air fryer basket and cook until soft, about 12 minutes.

2. Meanwhile, cut pita into triangles and separate each top and bottom layer to create 2 triangles.

3. Set the air fryer to 400ºF. Spray the pita triangles with cooking spray on both sides and place in the air fryer basket. Cook until dry and crisp, about 10 minutes, shaking or stirring twice during cooking.

4. Scoop out eggplant while hot and place flesh in food processor. Puree with curry powder until smooth. Drizzle in olive oil and season lightly. While blending, add garlic, honey, and vinegar. Transfer to a bowl and fold in scallions and olives. Check for flavor and season with additional salt and pepper, if necessary. Serve with pita chips.

WHOLE WHEAT PITA CHIPS
with Blackened Chive Dip

HERE'S ANOTHER RECIPE for homemade pita chips, this time with an out-of-this world dip made with blackened chives.

4-5 WHOLE WHEAT PITAS

COOKING SPRAY

EXTRA-VIRGIN OLIVE OIL, FOR COOKING

KOSHER SALT AND FRESHLY GROUND BLACK PEPPER

2 BUNCHES GARLIC CHIVES, CUT INTO 1/2-INCH PIECES

1 JALAPEÑO, MINCED

2 CUPS PLAIN NONFAT GREEK YOGURT

JUICE AND ZEST OF 1 LEMON

1. Cut pita into triangles and separate each top and bottom layer to create 2 triangles. Spray on all sides with cooking spray.

2. Set the air fryer to 400°F. Place pita triangles in the air fryer basket. Cook until dry and crisp, about 10 minutes, shaking or stirring twice during cooking.

3. Meanwhile, in a medium sauté pan over medium-high heat, add oil to coat the pan. Add garlic chives, season with salt and pepper, and cook until they turn dark brown or blacken. Remove from the heat and allow to cool slightly. In a bowl combine cooled chives, jalapeño, yogurt, and lemon juice and zest. Check for seasoning and serve with pita chips.

Air Fried GARLIC BREAD

IF YOU LOVE GARLIC KNOTS from your local pizza place, you'll love this fried garlic bread. Here, I use my family recipe for Chinese hot water dough, but if you want to go the easy route, simply buy a package of refrigerated pizza dough and skip steps 2 through 5.

1 HEAD GARLIC

COOKING SPRAY

2 CUPS WATER

4 CUPS ALL-PURPOSE FLOUR

1/2 TEASPOON SALT, PLUS MORE FOR SEASONING

1. Set air fryer to 375ºF. Leaving the skin on, slice off the very top of the garlic head, exposing the cloves inside. Spray exposed portion with a generous amount of cooking spray and wrap in aluminum foil. Place in air fryer basket and cook until cloves are soft, about 10 minutes. Keep warm in foil.

2. Meanwhile, bring the water to a boil. In a large stainless-steel bowl, combine flour and salt.

3. Slowly add boiling water in ¼-cup increments, mixing with chopsticks, until a ball is formed and dough is no longer too hot to handle. All the water may not be needed.

4. Knead dough on a floured work surface until it becomes smooth and elastic, 15 to 20 minutes.

5. Form dough into a ball, return it to the bowl, and cover with a damp cloth. Allow dough to rest for 1 hour.

6. Divide dough into ½-inch balls and stretch into thin ovals.

7. Set the air fryer to 350ºF. Working in batches, spray the dough ovals on all sides and lay them in a single layer in the air fryer basket. Cook for 5 minutes, check, and continue cooking until golden brown and delicious (GB&D) on both sides, about 3–5 more minutes. Repeat with remaining dough.

8. Remove garlic cloves from foil and immediately rub garlic onto bread. Sprinkle with salt. Serve.

BLUE GINGER *Crackers*

THIS RECIPE IS THE BASIS FOR THE DELICIOUS HOUSE CRACKERS at my restaurant Blue Ginger, but it can be used in a variety of ways depending on how you roll it out, from pretzel-like cracker sticks to pizza dough or anything you can dream up!

---

1 1/8 TEASPOONS ACTIVE DRY YEAST

1/2 CUP COLD WATER

1 1/2 CUPS BREAD FLOUR

1/4 CUP EXTRA-VIRGIN OLIVE OIL

2 TEASPOONS MINCED GARLIC

2 TEASPOONS KOSHER SALT

3/4 TEASPOON GROUND CUMIN

3/4 TEASPOON GROUND CORIANDER

3/4 TEASPOON GROUND FENNEL

3/4 TEASPOON GROUND BLACK PEPPER

COOKING SPRAY

1. In a 5-quart standing mixer bowl, or large bowl if working by hand, combine ingredients in this order: yeast, water, flour, oil, garlic, and salt. Using a dough hook, mix at low speed until the flour's gluten is fully developed and the dough is smooth and doesn't tear easily when stretched, about 15 minutes. Remove dough from the machine and knead in the spices by hand. (If working by hand, combine yeast, flour, oil, and salt and mound the mixture on a work surface. With your fingers, make a well in the mixture. Add water to the well and, working with a pastry scraper or large fork, gradually incorporate flour into the water 2 tablespoons at a time, as if you were making fresh pasta. Work dough into a rough ball and then knead in garlic and spice mixture. Continue to knead until the dough becomes smooth, 10 to 12 minutes.)

2. Cover dough with plastic wrap. If using immediately, allow the dough to rise in a warm place until doubled in bulk, about 1 hour.

3. Roll out dough on floured surface until ½-inch thick, then cut into circles using the bottom of a glass or cookie cutters. Or, cut into strips to make cracker sticks.

4. Set the air fryer to 400ºF. Working in batches, spray crackers on all sides with cooking spray and place in a single layer in the air fryer basket. Cook until golden brown, about 5 minutes. Repeat with remaining dough.

Scallion PANCAKES

SCALLION PANCAKES ARE A TRADITIONAL Chinese accompaniment, and can be enjoyed as an appetizer with dipping sauce, used as pita wraps or tortillas, or even be eaten as a meal on their own (especially if you stuff them with meat like my grandfather used to do). The possibilities are endless!

1 TABLESPOON SESAME OIL

3 TABLESPOONS EXTRA-VIRGIN OLIVE OIL

1 RECIPE HOT WATER DOUGH (PAGE 22)

2 CUPS SCALLIONS, WHITE AND GREEN PARTS, CUT DIAGONALLY INTO 1-INCH PIECES

KOSHER SALT AND

FRESHLY GROUND BLACK PEPPER

1 TABLESPOON GRAPESEED OR CANOLA OIL

1. In a small bowl, combine sesame and olive oils. Set aside.

2. Flour a work surface and roll out dough into a rectangle ⅛-inch thick. Brush dough with oil mixture, sprinkle with scallions, and season with salt and pepper. Starting with one long side nearest you, roll the dough jelly-roll fashion to make a tight log. Cut the log into 4 equal pieces.

3. Roll one piece with your palms to make a skinnier log about 12 inches long. Twist each end of the log in opposite directions 4 or 5 times (this will make additional pancake layers),

then wrap the log around itself to make a coil, tucking the outside end beneath the coil. With a rolling pin, flatten the coil to ¼-inch thick. Repeat with the remaining dough to make 3 more pancakes.

4. Set the air fryer to 400ºF. Working in batches, lay a scallion pancake flat in the air fryer basket. Cook for 4 minutes, flip, and continue cooking until brown and crispy, about 4 more minutes. Remove to serving plate and repeat with remaining pancakes.

5. Slice each pancake into 4 wedges. Serve with dipping sauce.

SPICY SOY DIPPING SAUCE

1 TABLESPOON SRIRACHA
SAUCE OR SAMBAL
(CHILE PASTE)

1/4 CUP RICE WINE
VINEGAR (PREFERABLY
NATURALLY BREWED)

1/4 CUP SOY SAUCE
(PREFERABLY NATURALLY
BREWED)

Combine all ingredients in a small bowl and serve.

SHALLOT *Pancakes*

THIS SPIN ON SCALLION PANCAKES is inspired by dim sum (Chinese brunch). They are great on their own, or with sautéed vegetables...especially mushrooms! They can even be used as a as a wrap or hamburger bun.

1 RECIPE HOT WATER DOUGH (PAGE 22)

1 TABLESPOON SESAME OIL

1/4 CUP CANOLA OIL

KOSHER SALT AND FRESHLY GROUND BLACK PEPPER

3 CUPS SLICED SHALLOTS

2 TABLESPOONS RAW SESAME SEEDS

1. Flour a work surface very lightly and roll out dough into a log. Cut log in half. Roll out one half-log very thinly (1/8-inch thick) into a large rectangle. In a small bowl, combine oils and brush over pancake and season with salt and pepper. Cover lightly with shallots.

2. Starting with one long side nearest you, roll the dough jelly-roll fashion to make a tight log. Twist each end of the log in opposite directions 4 or 5 times (this will make additional pancake layers), then wrap the log around itself to make a coil, tucking the outside end beneath the coil. With a rolling pin, flatten the coil to 1/4-inch thick, brush with additional oil mixture, and press sesame seeds into both sides. Repeat with remaining dough.

3. Set the air fryer to 400ºF. Working in batches, lay one pancake flat in the air fryer basket. Cook for 4 minutes, flip, and continue cooking until brown and crispy about 4 more minutes. Remove to serving plate and repeat with remaining pancake. Serve with Dim Sum Dipping Sauce.

Try it with...

DIM SUM DIPPING SAUCE

1/2 CUP SOY SAUCE (PREFERABLY NATURALLY BREWED)

1/4 CUP RICE VINEGAR (PREFERABLY NATURALLY BREWED)

1 TABLESPOON SRIRACHA SAUCE OR SAMBAL (CHILE PASTE)

1/2 BUNCH SCALLIONS, THINLY SLICED

Combine all ingredients in a bowl and serve.

SAUSAGE *Biscuits*

THESE SAVORY SAUSAGE BISCUITS ARE PERFECT for a snack, side, or even breakfast! Use roasted, minced garlic in a jar or use the instructions on page 22 to find out how to roast garlic in the air fryer. I like to make mine with Chinese sausage (lap chong) to give them an East-meets-West feel!

1 (8-OUNCE) TUBE REFRIGERATED CRESCENT ROLLS, OR 1/2 POUND MASTER DOUGHNUT DOUGH (PAGE 139)

1/4 CUP MINCED ROASTED GARLIC

1/4 CUP MINCED SAUSAGE

2 TABLESPOONS CHOPPED FRESH PARSLEY

1/2 CUP GRATED PARMIGIANO-REGGIANO CHEESE, PLUS SHAVED CHEESE, FOR GARNISH

COOKING SPRAY

1. On a clean work surface, lay out dough and press in garlic puree, sausage, parsley, and grated cheese until incorporated. Roll until well-incorporated. Roll out to ½-inch thick and cut dough into 1-inch rounds. Place on a parchment-lined or greased cookie sheet.

2. If using Master Doughnut Dough, preheat oven to 200ºF. When hot, turn oven off and place rounds, covered with a damp cloth, in oven. Let rise for about 30 minutes.

3. Set the air fryer to 400ºF. Spray rounds with cooking spray. Working in batches, place in a single layer in the air fryer basket. Cook until golden brown and delicious (GB&D), about 5 minutes, flipping halfway through cook time. Repeat with remaining dough. Garnish with shaved Parmigiano-Reggiano and serve immediately.

AMAZING
APPETIZERS

Air Fryer
ONION BLOSSOM

LIKE ONION RINGS, ONLY BETTER, an onion blossom is a delightful appetizer at parties that will go over equally well at a family dinner. Make sure to get a Vidalia onion (one of the big, squat-looking ones) which will get you that sweet onion-ring flavor you're looking for.

---

1 LARGE VIDALIA ONION, PEELED

1 CUP BUTTERMILK

2 LARGE EGGS

1 TEASPOON WATER

1¹/2 CUPS ALL-PURPOSE FLOUR

1/2 CUP FINE-GROUND CORNMEAL

1 TABLESPOON GARLIC POWDER

1 TABLESPOON SEASONED SALT

1 CUP PANKO (JAPANESE BREAD CRUMBS)

COOKING SPRAY

KOSHER SALT AND FRESHLY CRACKED PEPPER

---

1. Slice off the top of the onion, then make 12–14 downward slices into the onion, not cutting all the way through it, to make the onion "petals." Remove the center core and use the extra room to separate out each petal.

2. Submerge the onion in buttermilk (petal-side down) and refrigerate for 1 hour.

3. Beat eggs with water and set aside. Then combine the flour, cornmeal, garlic powder, and seasoned salt in a medium bowl. Remove the onion from the buttermilk and let the excess buttermilk drip off. Then dip it in the flour and then the egg. Sprinkle panko over top and shake to remove excess.

4. Set air fryer to 400 degrees. Spray onion petals all over with the cooking spray, then place in the air fryer basket. Cook until GB&D (golden brown and delicious), about 8–10 minutes.

Soy-Dijon CHICKEN WINGS

ONCE YOU TRY MAKING CHICKEN WINGS in the air fryer, you'll never want to make them any other way again! This mouthwatering version uses soy sauce and Dijon mustard for a rich and tangy taste.

---

1 TABLESPOON CRACKED BLACK PEPPERCORNS, PLUS FRESHLY GROUND BLACK PEPPER

1/4 CUP RED WINE

1/4 CUP PLUS 2 TABLESPOONS DIJON MUSTARD

2 TABLESPOONS SOY SAUCE (PREFERABLY NATURALLY BREWED)

2 SPRIGS FRESH THYME, CHOPPED, OR 2 TEASPOONS DRIED

2 TABLESPOONS MINCED GARLIC

KOSHER SALT

1/4 CUP CANOLA OIL

2 POUNDS CHICKEN WINGS, SEPARATED INTO DRUMETTES AND WINGS (TIPS DISCARDED)

1/4 CUP CRUMBLED BLUE CHEESE

CELERY STALKS, FOR SERVING

1. In a small, dry sauté pan, heat cracked peppercorns over medium-high heat, stirring, until fragrant and just beginning to smoke, 2 to 4 minutes.

2. Transfer to a medium nonreactive bowl and add wine, mustard, soy sauce, thyme, garlic, and salt to taste. Gradually whisk in oil to emulsify mixture. Set aside.

3. Pat wings dry with paper towels.

4. Set the air fryer to 400ºF. Place wings in the air fryer basket and cook for 20 to 25 minutes, stirring or shaking the basket every 5 minutes.

5. Remove wings with a flat strainer and transfer to a large bowl. Add the cheese to the marinade, add the mixture to the wings, and toss well. Serve immediately with celery.

Try it with...

CHINESE MUSTARD DIPPING SAUCE

1 TABLESPOON MUSTARD POWDER (PREFERABLY CHINESE MUSTARD)

3 TABLESPOONS CREME FRAÎCHE OR GREEK YOGURT

1 TABLESPOON HONEY

½ BUNCH CHIVES, CHOPPED

KOSHER SALT AND FRESHLY GROUND BLACK PEPPER

In a small bowl, add enough water to mustard powder to make a paste. Whisk in crème fraîche, honey, and chives. Season to taste with salt and pepper.

Fried SHRIMP BALLS

SHRIMP BALLS ARE AN IMPRESSIVE APPETIZER than everyone at your party will love—but don't let that keep you from just making a batch to enjoy at home. I've paired this recipe with a spin on vodka sauce made of soju, a unique-tasting Korean wine.

1½ POUNDS SHRIMP, PEELED AND DEVEINED

3 SHALLOTS, PEELED AND QUARTERED

1 SERRANO PEPPER OR 3 THAI BIRD CHILES

1 CUP UNSWEETENED SHREDDED COCONUT

1 TABLESPOON PACKED BROWN SUGAR

ZEST OF 2 LIMES, JUICE OF 1 LIME

KOSHER SALT AND FRESHLY GROUND BLACK PEPPER

1 CUP RICE FLOUR

1 TABLESPOON PAPRIKA

COOKING SPRAY

1. In a food processor, combine shrimp, shallots, chiles, coconut, brown sugar, lime zest, and lime juice. Process until well-combined; the mixture should have the consistency of ground meat. If too thin, add more coconut; if too thick, thin with lime juice and/or oil. Season lightly with salt and pepper.

2. Place rice flour in a shallow dish. With wet hands, mold shrimp mixture into balls.

3. Combine rice flour and paprika, and dredge shrimp balls in mixture. Spray with cooking spray.

4. Set air fryer to 400ºF and let preheat for 5 minutes.. Place shrimp balls in a single layer in the air fryer basket. Cook until golden brown, about 8 minutes. Remove from air fryer and allow to cool slightly. Salt lightly. Serve with Soju-Tomato Sauce.

Try it with...

SOJU-TOMATO SAUCE

1 (28-OUNCE) CAN ITALIAN PLUM TOMATOES (PREFERABLY SAN MARZANO), WITH THEIR LIQUID

1/4 CUP EXTRA-VIRGIN OLIVE OIL

8 SMASHED GARLIC CLOVES

KOSHER SALT

RED PEPPER FLAKES, TO TASTE

1/4 CUP SOJU OR VODKA

1/2 CUP HEAVY CREAM

2 TABLESPOONS UNSALTED BUTTER OR EXTRA-VIRGIN OLIVE OIL, FOR FINISHING (OPTIONAL)

Pulse tomatoes and their liquid in a food processor until finely chopped. Heat olive oil in a large skillet over medium heat and add garlic cloves. Cook, shaking the skillet, until garlic is lightly browned, about 3 minutes. Add tomatoes to the pan. Bring to a boil, season with salt and red pepper, and boil for about 2 minutes. Add soju and simmer for about 8 minutes. Remove garlic cloves from sauce and add cream. Add butter, if using, and stir to incorporate. Check for flavor.

Chicken "MOO SHU-QUITOS"

A "MOO SHU-QUITO" IS A COMBINATION of moo shu, a Chinese dish featuring mushrooms, and taquitos, crispy Mexican roll-ups. Sure, I just made the word up, but you'll forgive me when you taste these appetizers that are packed with flavor.

GRAPESEED OR CANOLA OIL, FOR COOKING

1 POUND BUTTON MUSHROOMS, SLICED

1 LARGE YELLOW ONION, SLICED

KOSHER SALT AND FRESHLY CRACKED BLACK PEPPER

1 1/2 POUNDS COOKED CHICKEN, CUT INTO 1/2-INCH STRIPS

1/2 POUND WHITE CHEDDAR CHEESE, SHREDDED

10 MEDIUM FLOUR TORTILLAS OR MOO SHU WRAPPERS

COOKING SPRAY

1 CUP SALSA, FOR SERVING

1. In a medium sauté pan coated lightly with oil over medium-high heat, add mushrooms and onions. Season with salt and pepper. Cook for 10 to 12 minutes, until slightly browned and most of the moisture has evaporated. Transfer to a chilled sheet tray to cool to room temperature.

2. In a large bowl, mix cooled mushroom mixture with chicken and cheese. Lay out tortillas or moo shu wrappers, spoon chicken mixture down middle of wrapper, and roll up very tightly (both ends will be open).

3. Set the air fryer to 400ºF. Working in batches if necessary, place the moo shu-quitos seam-side down in a single layer in the air fryer basket. Spray with cooking spray. Cook until GB&D (golden brown and delicious), about 6 minutes. Repeat with remaining moo shu-quitos. Serve sliced diagonally, topped with salsa.

FRIED *Shrimp*

FRIED SHRIMP IS A COMMON APPETIZER at Japanese restaurants, but it's also a tasty lunch or dinner. To make sure they fry up nice 'n' crispy, I've added panko bread crumbs to this version. Try them in my Shrimp, Yogurt, and Couscous Parfait on page 49.

1 CUP RICE FLOUR, PLUS SOME EXTRA IF NEEDED

1½ TEASPOONS GROUND CORIANDER

1½ TEASPOONS GROUND CUMIN

3/4 TEASPOON GROUND BLACK PEPPER

4 LARGE SHRIMP, PEELED AND DEVEINED

1 LARGE EGG, BEATEN

3/4 CUP PANKO (JAPANESE BREAD CRUMBS)

COOKING SPRAY

KOSHER SALT AND FRESHLY GROUND BLACK PEPPER

1. In a large bowl, combine rice flour, coriander, cumin, and pepper. Dredge shrimp in mixture until fully covered.

2. Dip shrimp in egg, allowing the excess to drip off. Then cover thoroughly with panko. Spray on all sides with cooking spray.

3. Set air fryer to 400°F. Place shrimp in a single layer in the air fryer basket. Cook until GB&D (golden brown and delicious), about 8–10 minutes. Remove from air fryer to a plate and lightly season with salt and pepper. Serve with Lemon Aioli.

Try it with...

LEMON AIOLI

2 TEASPOONS MINCED GARLIC

2 EGG YOLKS

1/2 CUP PLUS
2 TABLESPOONS
GRAPESEED OIL

JUICE OF 1 LEMON

KOSHER SALT AND
FRESHLY GROUND
BLACK PEPPER

In a food processor, combine garlic and yolks and blend until smooth and yolks are pale and creamy. With food processor running, very slowly drizzle in oil. You want an emulsification to form, so go slowly; once about a quarter of the oil has been added, you can pour the rest in a steady stream. Add lemon juice and blend briefly. Season with salt and pepper.

Shrimp, Yogurt, and
COUSCOUS PARFAIT

THIS FANCY APPETIZER IS SERVED in a martini glass, but don't let its impressive appearance fool you. Once you've made some panko-crusted shrimp (page 46) it's easy to combine with Greek yogurt and couscous to make an hors d'oeuvre that will win raves.

1 SHALLOT, MINCED

1 TEASPOON MADRAS CURRY POWDER

1 TEASPOON MINCED GINGER

2 CUPS NONFAT GREEK YOGURT

2 CUPS COOKED COUSCOUS

JUICE AND ZEST OF 1 LARGE LIME

EXTRA-VIRGIN OLIVE OIL, TO COOK AND TO DRIZZLE

KOSHER SALT AND FRESHLY GROUND BLACK PEPPER

8 LARGE FRIED SHRIMP (SEE PAGE 46)

1. In a small bowl, mix together shallot, curry powder, ginger, and yogurt, and season to taste with salt and pepper. Set mixture aside.

2. In a separate bowl, mix couscous with lime juice and zest, drizzle with oil, and season with salt and pepper.

3. Make parfaits in martini glasses by layering yogurt, then couscous, and then another layer of yogurt. Place 2 shrimp on top of each parfait.

MOZZARELLA *Sticks*

WHAT'S BETTER THAN MOZZARELLA STICKS? Homemade mozzarella sticks from your air fryer! This version uses string cheese and is super-easy to make.

1 (12-OUNCE) PACKAGE MOZZARELLA STRING CHEESE

1/4 CUP ALL-PURPOSE FLOUR

2 LARGE EGGS, BEATEN

2 CUPS BREAD CRUMBS

1 TABLESPOON DRIED OREGANO

2 TEASPOONS SALT

1 TEASPOON BLACK PEPPER

1/4 CUP FRESHLY GRATED PARMESAN CHEESE

COOKING SPRAY

1. Remove cheese from the individually wrapped packages and stack on a cutting board. With a sharp knife, slice sticks in half, or thirds, depending on the size you like. Place cheese on a parchment paper–lined cookie sheet, cover in plastic wrap, and freeze for 2 hours.

2. In a shallow dish, mix together bread crumbs, oregano, salt, pepper, and Parmesan. Place flour and eggs in two other shallow dishes.

3. Immediately upon removing cheese sticks from the freezer, roll them first in flour, then in beaten eggs, and lastly in the bread crumb mixture. As you prepare them, place them on the cookie sheet you used to freeze them until they're all ready. Spray sticks with cooking spray.

4. Set air fryer to 400ºF. Place sticks in the air fryer basket, making sure they don't touch.

5. Cook for 3 minutes, flip, and continuing cooking until golden brown and delicious, an additional 3 to 4 minutes.

Air-Fried RAVIOLI

JUST ABOUT EVERYTHING IS BETTER AIR-FRIED, and ravioli is no exception. Make these for a party and they'll become an instant classic; they're equally as good for a quick dinner or lunch.

1 CUP PANKO (JAPANESE BREAD CRUMBS)

2 TABLESPOONS DRIED OREGANO

1 TABLESPOON DRIED BASIL

1 TEASPOON SALT

1 TEASPOON FRESHLY GROUND BLACK PEPPER

2 EGGS BEATEN WITH 2 TABLESPOONS WATER FOR EGG WASH

1 CUP ALL-PURPOSE FLOUR

1 (9-OUNCE) PACKAGE REFRIGERATED RAVIOLI

COOKING SPRAY

MARINARA SAUCE, FOR SERVING

1. In a medium bowl, combine panko, oregano, basil, salt, and pepper. Place egg wash and flour in separate bowls.

2. Dredge each ravioli with flour, then dip it in egg wash and cover thoroughly with panko mixture.

3. Set air fryer to 400ºF. Working in batches, spray ravioli on all sides with cooking spray. Cook until GB&D (golden brown and delicious), about 5–6 minutes. Repeat with remaining ravioli. Serve with marinara sauce for dipping.

Caramelized Shallot and Pork
SPRING ROLLS

WHEN YOU ORDER FROM A CHINESE RESTAURANT, I bet you order the egg rolls, right? Also called "spring rolls," they're easy to make at home in the air fryer! Just keep an eye out for egg roll wrappers, which can be found in the refrigerated (or sometimes frozen) foods section of your grocery store.

---

2 TABLESPOONS BUTTER

5-6 MEDIUM SHALLOTS, CHOPPED

1 POUND GROUND PORK

1 CUP SHREDDED CARROTS

KOSHER SALT AND FRESHLY GROUND BLACK PEPPER

8-12 REFRIGERATED OR FROZEN EGG ROLL WRAPS, THAWED

COOKING SPRAY

RED LEAF LETTUCE, PREFERABLY THE TENDER INNER LEAVES, FOR SERVING

1. In small saucepan, melt butter, then sauté shallots until soft. Cover and let caramelize, stirring occasionally, about 15 minutes.

2. In a large bowl, mix shallots, pork, and carrots and season with salt and pepper. (If desired, check seasoning by microwaving or sautéing a small portion of the filling.)

3. Lay out egg roll wrappers on a flat surface, top with pork mix, roll tightly, and let rest, seam-side down, for a little less than a minute. Repeat with remaining wrappers.

4. Set air fryer to 325ºF. Working in batches, spray the outsides of each spring roll with cooking spray and place seam-side down in a single layer in the air fryer basket. Cook until GB&D (golden brown and delicious), about 15 minutes, turning once during cook time. Repeat with remaining rolls.

5. Serve spring rolls on lettuce leaves accompanied by Carrot Dipping Sauce.

Try it with...

CARROT DIPPING SAUCE

1/4 CUP FISH SAUCE

JUICE OF 4 LIMES

2 TEASPOONS SUGAR

1/2 SERRANO PEPPER OR
2 FRESH THAI BIRD
CHILES, MINCED

2 TABLESPOONS
SHREDDED CARROTS

In a small bowl, stir together fish sauce, lime juice, sugar, chiles, and carrots.

PESTO CHICKEN AND SPINACH *Spring Rolls*

PESTO IS USUALLY PAIRED WITH PASTA, but it tastes equally great in spring rolls! Use ground chicken in this recipe, or finely chop some leftover chicken to turn yesterday's dinner into today's appetizers.

1 POUND GROUND CHICKEN BREAST

3 CUPS FRESH BABY SPINACH, FINELY CHOPPED

1 CUP SHREDDED CARROTS

1 PINT PESTO SAUCE

8-12 REFRIGERATED OR FROZEN EGG ROLL WRAPS, THAWED

1 EGG BEATEN WITH 1 TABLESPOON WATER FOR EGG WASH

1. Fill a bowl with ice and place another bowl with the chicken on top of the ice. Add chopped spinach, carrots, and three-quarters of the pesto. Mix together. Season with salt and pepper. (If desired, check seasoning by microwaving or sautéing a small portion of the filling.)

2. Lay out egg roll wrappers, top with chicken mixture, roll tightly, and let rest seam-side down. Repeat with remaining wrappers.

3. Set the air fryer to 400ºF. Working in batches, place spring rolls seam-side down in a single layer in the air fryer basket. Brush with egg wash. Cook until golden brown and delicious (GB&D), 6 to 8 minutes. Repeat with remaining rolls. Cut spring rolls in half diagonally before serving.

TURKEY *Spring Rolls*

THE COMBO OF GARLIC AND GINGER IS AN ASIAN CLASSIC, and using ground turkey instead of ground beef in these spring rolls is a great way to save calories (but you can always use ground beef instead, if you want!).

2 TABLESPOONS CANOLA OIL

2 RED ONIONS, SLICED

4 CLOVES GARLIC, MINCED

1 TABLESPOON MINCED GINGER

2 CARROTS, SHREDDED

1 POUND GROUND TURKEY (PREFERABLY DARK MEAT)

KOSHER SALT AND FRESHLY GROUND BLACK PEPPER

16 REFRIGERATED OR FROZEN EGG ROLL WRAPS, THAWED

1 EGG BEATEN WITH 1 TABLESPOON WATER FOR EGG WASH

1. In a large, preferably cast-iron skillet, heat oil over medium-high heat. Add red onion, garlic, and ginger and cook, stirring occasionally, until softened, about 8 minutes. Allow to cool, and transfer mixture to a large bowl. Add shredded carrots, ground turkey, salt, and pepper, and combine well. Check seasoning by microwaving or sautéing a small portion of the filling.

2. To form the spring rolls, spread about ¼ cup filling across one corner of the wrapper. Roll on the diagonal toward the center, tucking in the corner as you go. Stop at the halfway point and paint the two edges of the square with egg wash. Fold the sides in toward the center and continue rolling all the way. Rest roll, seam-side down, and repeat with additional filling and wrappers.

3. Set the air fryer to 400ºF. Working in batches, place spring rolls seam-side down in a single layer in the air fryer basket. Brush with egg wash. Cook until golden brown and delicious (GB&D), 6 to 8 minutes. Repeat with remaining rolls. Cut in half diagonally (or leave whole) and serve with Hoisin-Lime Dipping Sauce.

Try it with...

HOISIN-LIME DIPPING SAUCE

3 TABLESPOONS CANOLA OIL

1 CLOVE GARLIC, SLICED

1/2 TEASPOON MINCED GINGER

1/3 CUP HOISIN SAUCE

JUICE OF 1 LIME

In a small saucepan, heat oil over medium-high heat. Add garlic and ginger and stir until fragrant, about 30 seconds, then add hoisin sauce. Cook, stirring frequently, until sauce loses some of its raw flavor, about 4 minutes. Remove from the heat. Squeeze in lime juice, stir to combine, and serve.

Seafood LUMPIAS

"LUMPIAS" ARE WHAT THEY CALL SPRING ROLLS in the Philippines and Indonesia, so using seafood inside is the perfect fit. These taste great with this divine Citrus-Mint Syrup or with my other spring roll sauces.

---

1 POUND SMALL SHRIMP, PEELED AND DEVEINED

1/2 POUND BLACK COD (SABLEFISH) OR SEA BASS, FILLET, CUT INTO 1-INCH DICE

1/2 POUND BAY SCALLOPS

1 EGG

1 TABLESPOON FINELY CHOPPED FRESH GINGER

1/2 CUP THINLY SLICED SCALLIONS

1/4 CUP CHOPPED FRESH CILANTRO

1 TEASPOON TOASTED SESAME OIL

KOSHER SALT AND FRESHLY GROUND BLACK PEPPER

16–20 REFRIGERATED OR FROZEN LUMPIA WRAPPERS OR EGG ROLL WRAPS, THAWED

1 EGG BEATEN WITH 1/4 CUP WATER FOR EGG WASH

1. In a food processor, combine shrimp, fish, scallops, egg, ginger, scallions, cilantro, and sesame oil. Pulse to finely chop; do not puree. Check for flavor by microwaving or sautéing a small portion and season with salt and pepper as needed.

2. Have a small bowl of water handy to wet your fingertips. Place a lumpia wrapper on a work surface with a corner near you. Place about 2 tablespoons of filling a little above the corner and bring the near corner of the wrapper over the filling to enclose it. Brush the edges with egg wash, roll tightly toward the middle of the wrapper, then fold in the sides and continue to roll to make a sticklike spring roll, as thin as possible, ideally ¼- to ½-inch in diameter. Rest roll seam-side down and repeat with remaining wrappers and filling.

3. Set the air fryer to 350ºF. Working in batches, place lumpias seam-side down in a single layer in the air fryer basket. Cook until GB&D (golden brown and delicious), 8 to 10 minutes. Repeat with remaining lumpias. To serve, stand lumpias in a large glass and serve with a dipping bowl of Citrus-Mint Syrup.

Try it with...

CITRUS-MINT SYRUP

1 TABLESPOON SOY SAUCE
(PREFERABLY NATURALLY
BREWED)

JUICE OF 2 MEDIUM
ORANGES

JUICE OF 1 LEMON

JUICE OF 2 LIMES

1 TABLESPOON DIJON
MUSTARD

1/4 CUP FRESH
MINT LEAVES

KOSHER SALT AND
FRESHLY GROUND
BLACK PEPPER

1/4 CUP GRAPESEED
OR CANOLA OIL

In a medium nonreactive saucepan, combine soy sauce and juices and bring to a boil over medium heat. Reduce heat and simmer until mixture is reduced by half, 10 to 12 minutes. Cool to room temperature. Transfer soy-citrus mixture to a blender, add mustard and mint, and season with salt and pepper. Blend on high until incorporated, then carefully remove plastic plug in top of blender. Slowly add in grapeseed oil, forming an emulsion. Check for flavor, season if necessary, and store in the refrigerator in an airtight container.

Zucchini CROQUETTES

ZUCCHINI DOESN'T HAVE TO BE BORING! These crispy, tasty bites prove it. Serve them with some marinara sauce for dipping.

1 MEDIUM ZUCCHINI, PEELED AND GRATED

1/4 CUP RICOTTA CHEESE

1 LARGE EGG, BEATEN

1/2 TEASPOON KOSHER SALT

1/4 TEASPOON FRESHLY GROUND BLACK PEPPER

1 GARLIC CLOVE, MINCED

2 SCALLIONS, WHITE AND GREEN PARTS, FINELY CHOPPED

1/2 CUP PANKO (JAPANESE BREAD CRUMBS)

COOKING SPRAY

1. In a medium bowl, combine zucchini, ricotta, egg, salt, and pepper in a bowl and mix until combined. Mix in garlic and scallions, then fold in bread crumbs.

2. Scoop about 2 tablespoons of the mixture into the palm of your hand. Roll into a ball, and spray on all sides with cooking spray. Repeat with remaining mixture.

3. Set air fryer to 400ºF. Working in batches, place croquettes in a single layer in the air fryer basket, leaving space between each one. Cook for 7 to 8 minutes. Repeat with remaining croquettes.

Mama Tsai's Party Curry
BEEF PINWHEELS

MY MOM'S CURRY BEEF PINWHEELS might be my favorite appetizer of all time—although, in all fairness, they're just as good for lunch or even dinner. They're filling, flavorful, and look almost like a (meaty) cinnamon roll when you're done! Just make sure not to skip the freezing step; it helps keep the pinwheels together.

---

1 TABLESPOON CANOLA OIL

1 LARGE ONION, MINCED

1 POUND GROUND BEEF

2 TEASPOONS CURRY POWDER

1/8 TEASPOON GROUND GINGER

KOSHER SALT AND FRESHLY GROUND BLACK PEPPER

2 TABLESPOONS CORNSTARCH

2 TABLESPOONS WATER

2 TABLESPOONS MINCED CILANTRO, PLUS SOME SPRIGS FOR GARNISH

2 PACKAGES FROZEN UNSWEETENED PIE DOUGH

2 TEASPOONS GRAPESEED OR CANOLA OIL

COOKING SPRAY

1. In a wok or sauté pan coated lightly with oil, sauté onions until soft and translucent, about 2 to 3 minutes.

2. Add beef and season with curry powder, ginger, salt, and pepper. Cook until browned, about 4 to 5 minutes.

3. In a small bowl, combine water and cornstarch until you make a watery paste. Add to pan, and stir to thicken beef mixture. Transfer to a mixing bowl and fold in cilantro. Cover and refrigerate for 10 minutes.

4. Roll out the pie dough and until it's 1/8-inch thick. Brush a thin layer of oil on dough and place a thin layer of meat filling on top. Beginning at one end, roll into a log, with layers of the meat on the inside. Freeze overnight or up to 1 month.

5. Remove from the freezer and slice into 1/2-inch-thick discs. Spray the outsides with cooking spray.

6. Set air fryer to 350ºF. Line air fryer basket with parchment paper. Working in batches, place curry beef pinwheels in a single layer in the air fryer basket. Cook, until golden brown, 10–12 minutes. Serve hot, garnished with cilantro sprigs.

DELECTABLE DINNERS

Pepperoni MINI PIZZAS

PEPPERONI PIZZA IS THE ULTIMATE KID FOOD—give these to your clan and "mini pizzas!" is probably what you'll hear from them when you say "What do you want to dinner?" for at least a few months. These are so quick and easy to make, though, that you may find it becomes *your* favorite dinner as well! They're also ideal for an after-school or after-work snack.

---

1 (16.3-OUNCE) TUBE OF REFRIGERATED BISCUIT ROUNDS

1/2 CUP PIZZA SAUCE

1 CUP MOZZARELLA CHEESE, GRATED

1 PACKAGE PEPPERONI

10-12 GRAPE OR CHERRY TOMATOES, HALVED

1. Flatten biscuit rounds to ¼-inch thick. Top with pizza sauce, cheese, pepperoni, and tomatoes.

2. Set air fryer to 350ºF. Working in batches, place pizzas in single layer in air fryer basket. Cook until cheese is melted and dough is cooked, about 8–10 minutes.

Spicy Barbecue
CHICKEN PIZZAS

ADD SOME ASIAN SPICE to your favorite barbecue sauce in these crafty air-fried pizzas, and you don't even need pizza sauce! Add the scallions after the pizzas are done cooking if you prefer them crunchy.

1 (16.3-OUNCE) TUBE OF REFRIGERATED BISCUIT ROUNDS

1 CUP COOKED CHICKEN, CHOPPED

1/4 CUP BARBECUE SAUCE

1 TABLESPOON SAMBAL OR SRIRACHA SAUCE

KOSHER SALT AND FRESHLY GROUND BLACK PEPPER

1 CUP GRUYÈRE OR MOZZARELLA CHEESE, GRATED

2 SCALLIONS, CHOPPED

1. In a large bowl, mix together chicken, barbecue sauce, and sambal or Sriracha. Season with salt and pepper.

2. Flatten biscuit rounds to ¼-inch thick. Top with cheese, chicken mixture, and scallions.

3. Set air fryer to 350ºF. Working in batches, place pizzas in single layer in air fryer basket. Cook until cheese is melted and dough is cooked, about 8–10 minutes.

SPICY CHICKEN *Sambal*

IF YOU LOVE "ROOSTER SAUCE," you'll love this take on chicken with a spicy marinade made with orange juice to give it both sweetness and a bright acidity.

1/4 + 1 TABLESPOON SAMBAL OR SRIRACHA SAUCE

1 TABLESPOON DIJON MUSTARD

2 TABLESPOONS WORCESTERSHIRE SAUCE

JUICE OF 1 ORANGE

2 BONELESS CHICKEN BREAST HALVES

COOKING SPRAY

KOSHER SALT AND FRESHLY GROUND BLACK PEPPER

1. In a large bowl, combine sambal or Sriracha, mustard, and Worcestershire sauce. Whisk in orange juice. Season chicken on both sides with salt and add to marinade. Cover and refrigerate for 30 minutes.

2. Set the air fryer to 400°F. Remove chicken from marinade and shake of excess. Place chicken breasts in the air fryer basket and cook until juices run clear when chicken is pricked with the tip of a knife in its thickest part, about 10 minutes.

SHALLOT-SOY *Chicken*

THE VINEGAR IN THIS MARINADE helps tenderize as well as flavor the chicken, but it also makes a delicious salad dressing when eaten on its own (just make sure to use a version that *hasn't* touched raw meat, naturally). Better yet, save some for a salad to eat on the side.

1/4 CUP GRAINY MUSTARD

2 MEDIUM SHALLOTS, FINELY CHOPPED

1 TABLESPOON BALSAMIC OR CHINESE BLACK VINEGAR

2 TABLESPOONS RICE WINE VINEGAR (PREFERABLY NATURALLY BREWED)

1 TABLESPOON SOY SAUCE (PREFERABLY NATURALLY BREWED)

2 TEASPOONS SUGAR

1/2 CUP GRAPESEED OR CANOLA OIL

1/2 TEASPOON KOSHER SALT

1/2 TEASPOON FRESHLY GROUND BLACK PEPPER

4 LARGE BONELESS CHICKEN BREAST HALVES

1. In a large bowl, combine mustard, shallots, vinegars, soy sauce, and sugar and stir vigorously until sugar is dissolved. While stirring, slowly drizzle in oil until an emulsion is formed. Season with salt and pepper.

2. Add chicken and toss to coat. Cover and marinate, refrigerated, at least 1 hour and up to 4 hours.

3. Set the air fryer to 400ºF. Working in batches, place 2 chicken breasts in the air fryer basket, and cook until juices run clear when chicken is pricked with the tip of a knife in its thickest part, about 10 minutes. Remove and let chicken rest for 5 minutes. Repeat with remaining breasts. Serve with a side salad, if desired.

Ham-Wrapped CHICKEN

ONE OF THE BEST WAYS TO SEASON MEAT is with more meat! This ham-wrapped chicken is great with some sliced ham from your deli counter, but if you want you can get more fancy and serve it with prosciutto or my favorite, Spanish jamón ibérico de Fermin.

---

4 BONELESS CHICKEN BREAST HALVES

KOSHER SALT AND FRESHLY GROUND BLACK PEPPER

16 LARGE BASIL LEAVES

8 SLICES HAM

1. Season chicken breasts with salt and pepper. Cover each breast with 4 basil leaves, then wrap in ham. Secure with a toothpick.

2. Set the air fryer to 400ºF. Working in batches, place 2 chicken breasts in the air fryer basket and cook until the juices run clear when chicken is pricked with the tip of a knife in its thickest part, about 10 minutes. Once chicken is done, remove from air fryer and serve.

LEMONGRASS *Chicken*

THIS DELICATELY FLAVORED CHICKEN is wonderful for adding something different into your weekly chicken routine. If you can't find lemongrass at a nearby Asian market, simply substitute the zest of a lemon and, if desired, a pinch of minced ginger.

4 BONELESS CHICKEN BREAST HALVES

5 STALKS LEMONGRASS, MINCED (WHITE PART ONLY)

2 SHALLOTS, MINCED

1/2 CUP WHITE WINE

3 TABLESPOONS EXTRA-VIRGIN OLIVE OIL, DIVIDED

KOSHER SALT AND FRESHLY GROUND BLACK PEPPER

1/4 CUP CHOPPED KALAMATA OLIVES

COUSCOUS, FOR SERVING

1. In a large zip-top bag, combine chicken, lemongrass, shallots, wine, and 2 tablespoons olive oil and marinate for 30 minutes. Remove marinated chicken to a plate and season with salt and pepper. Reserve marinade for pan sauce.

2. Set the air fryer to 400ºF. Working in batches, place 2 chicken breasts in the air fryer basket. Cook until the juices run clear when chicken is pricked with the tip of a knife in its thickest part, about 10 minutes. Remove and let chicken rest 5 minutes. Repeat with remaining breasts.

3. Transfer remaining marinade to a small saucepan and bring to a boil. Add olives and remaining tablespoon olive oil, stir to combine, and heat through. Serve family-style by placing chicken breasts over couscous. Garnish by spooning pan sauce over chicken.

SPICY CRISPY *Chicken Tenders*

THE SMOKY SPICINESS OF THESE CHICKEN FINGERS take them from the kids' table to bona fide adult food—but, of course, you can always remove the chile powder and make some for the kids.

---

1 CUP PANKO (JAPANESE BREAD CRUMBS)

2 TABLESPOONS KOCHU KARU (KOREAN CHILE POWDER) OR CHIPOTLE CHILE POWDER

2 LARGE BONELESS CHICKEN BREASTS HALVES, CUT INTO LONG STRIPS

KOSHER SALT AND FRESHLY GROUND BLACK PEPPER

1/2 CUP ALL-PURPOSE FLOUR

2 LARGE EGGS, BEATEN

COOKING SPRAY

CHOPPED SCALLIONS OR CHIVES, FOR GARNISH

1. Combine panko and chile powder on a plate. Set aside.

2. Season chicken slices with salt and pepper, dredge in flour, then dip in egg, letting excess drip off. Next, dip in panko, covering thoroughly. Spray chicken on all sides with cooking spray.

3. Set the air fryer to 350ºF. Place the chicken strips in the air fryer basket and cook for until GB&D (golden brown and delicious), 10 to 12 minutes. Remove from air fryer, garnish with scallions, and serve with your favorite condiment.

Coconut CHICKEN TENDERS

THESE CRUNCHY CHICKEN TENDERS have a bit of sweetness that make them irresistible. Try them with your favorite salsa!

1/2 CUP PANKO (JAPANESE BREAD CRUMBS)

1/2 CUP SWEETENED COCONUT FLAKES

2 TABLESPOONS FINELY CHOPPED CASHEWS

2 TABLESPOONS ALL-PURPOSE FLOUR

1 TABLESPOON BROWN SUGAR

2 TEASPOONS SALT

2 LARGE BONELESS CHICKEN BREASTS HALVES, CUT INTO LONG STRIPS

KOSHER SALT AND FRESHLY GROUND BLACK PEPPER

1 CUP PLAIN GREEK YOGURT

COOKING SPRAY

KOSHER SALT AND FRESHLY GROUND BLACK PEPPER

1. Combine panko, coconut flakes, cashews, flour, brown sugar, and salt on a plate. Set aside.

2. Season chicken slices with salt and pepper, then coat thoroughly with yogurt, letting excess drip off. Next, dip in panko mixture, covering thoroughly. Spray chicken on all sides with cooking spray.

3. Set the air fryer to 400ºF. Place the chicken strips in the air fryer basket and cook for until GB&D (golden brown and delicious), 8 to 10 minutes. Remove from air fryer, and season lightly before serving.

THAI CURRY *Fried Chicken*

IF YOU'VE NEVER TRIED THAI CURRY PASTE, now is the time to head over to the Asian section of your supermarket. Sold in small jars, this flavor-packed seasoning is available in three (sometimes more) varieties: yellow (the most mild and richest curry), red (a bright, hot curry), and green (even hotter curry that also has a sweetness to it). Pick your favorite and use it in sauces, coconut milk stir-frys, and this must-try recipe.

---

2 1/2 POUNDS CHICKEN (ABOUT 1 SMALL), SKIN ON, BROKEN INTO PARTS

KOSHER SALT AND FRESHLY GROUND PEPPER

4 LARGE EGGS

1 TABLESPOON MILK OR BUTTERMILK

2 TEASPOONS THAI CURRY PASTE

1 1/2 CUPS ALL-PURPOSE FLOUR

1/2 CUP WHEAT FLOUR

1 TABLESPOON BAKING POWDER

1 TEASPOON KOSHER SALT

COOKING SPRAY

1. Season chicken pieces with salt and pepper. In a large bowl, combine eggs, milk or buttermilk, and thai curry paste. Whisk to combine. Separately, combine flours, baking powder, and salt and place on a plate.

2. Dip each chicken piece in egg mixture, then flour. Spray on all sides with cooking spray.

3. Set the air fryer to 350ºF. Working in batches, place chicken in a single layer in the air fryer basket. Cook for 25 minutes, turning once and spraying with more cooking spray halfway through cooking time. Increase air fryer to 400º and turn and spray with cooking spray once more. Cook until golden, brown and delicious (GB&D) and internal temperature is 165ºF, about 10 minutes. Remove chicken to paper towel–lined plate and season immediately with salt. Repeat with remaining chicken. Enjoy!

PERFECT *Crispy Chicken* SANDWICH

HERE IT IS: My not-so-secret-anymore recipe for a perfectly spiced crispy chicken sandwich. One of my most popular dishes at my restaurant Blue Ginger, this sandwich has everything going for it, from the soft bun that absorbs all the juices, to the perfect mixture of mustard and mayo to accompany it, and my favorite—crispy Japanese bread crumbs, which I've spiced here with thyme, basil, ginger, and chile.

---

2 CUPS PANKO (JAPANESE BREAD CRUMBS)

1 TABLESPOON DRIED THYME

1 TABLESPOON DRIED BASIL

1 1/2 TEASPOONS POWDERED GINGER

1 1/2 TEASPOONS COARSELY GROUND BLACK PEPPER

1 1/2 TEASPOONS ANCHO CHILE POWDER OR REGULAR CHILE POWDER

1 CUP ALL-PURPOSE FLOUR

3 EGGS, LIGHTLY BEATEN

4 LARGE BONELESS, SKINLESS CHICKEN BREASTS, POUNDED AS NEEDED FOR CONSISTENT THICKNESS

KOSHER SALT AND FRESHLY GROUND BLACK PEPPER

2 TABLESPOONS DIJON MUSTARD

1/4 CUP MAYONNAISE

4 SESAME SEED BUNS, SPLIT

1 HEAD ICEBERG LETTUCE, SHREDDED

1 LARGE RIPE TOMATO, CORED AND SLICED 1/4-INCH THICK

1. In a medium bowl, combine panko, thyme, basil, ginger, pepper, and chile powder. Place flour, eggs, and panko in 3 separate shallow dishes.

2. Season chicken breasts with salt and pepper. Dredge them in flour, shaking off the excess. Dip in eggs and then panko.

3. Set the air fryer to 350ºF. Working in batches, place chicken in a single layer in the air fryer basket. Cook until golden brown and its juices run clear when pricked with the tip of a knife, 10 to 12 minutes.

4. Meanwhile, in a small bowl, combine mustard and mayonnaise. To assemble sandwiches, spread mustard mixture lightly on bun tops and bottoms. Top the bottoms with lettuce, one chicken breast, and tomatoes. Season tomatoes with salt and pepper, and cover with bun tops. Halve each sandwich and serve.

Turkey SCALOPPINI

SCALOPPINI IS A FANCY WAY OF SAYING breaded slices of meat. It originates in Italy, and is perfect for serving with tomato sauce. If you're in the Thanksgiving mood, however, you can try it with my Cranberry Mango Vinaigrette.

---

1 BONELESS, SKINLESS TURKEY BREAST, SLICED INTO 1/2-INCH PIECES

KOSHER SALT AND FRESHLY GROUND BLACK PEPPER

1 CUP PANKO (JAPANESE BREAD CRUMBS)

1/2 CUP CHOPPED PARSLEY, DIVIDED

1 CUP ALL-PURPOSE FLOUR

2 EGGS, LIGHTLY BEATEN

1. Place a sheet of plastic wrap over each turkey slice, and pound to about ¼-inch thick. Season both sides with salt and pepper.

2. In a shallow dish, combine panko and half the parsley. Place eggs and flour in two other shallow dishes. Dust each turkey slice in flour, dredge in egg, then coat in panko.

3. Set air fryer to 375ºF. Working in batches, place turkey slices in a single layer in the air fryer basket. Cook until GB&D (golden brown and delicious), 12 to 15 minutes. Serve with Cranberry-Mango Vinaigrette or tomato sauce drizzled on top.

Try it with...

CRANBERRY-MANGO VINAIGRETTE

2 SHALLOTS, ROUGH
CHOPPED

JUICE OF 1 LEMON

1 TABLESPOON DIJON
MUSTARD

2 CUPS FRESH
CRANBERRIES

1/2 CUP DRIED
CRANBERRIES

1 LARGE MANGO, PEELED
AND DICED

KOSHER SALT AND
FRESHLY CRACKED BLACK
PEPPER

1/2 CUP EXTRA-VIRGIN
OLIVE OIL

In a blender, combine shallots, lemon juice, and Dijon mustard and puree until smooth. Add cranberries and mango and puree until smooth. Season with salt and pepper to taste. With blender running, slowly drizzle in olive oil and taste again. Store leftovers in an airtight container in the refrigerator.

Crispy Potato-Crusted SHRIMP

IF YOU THINK INSTANT POTATO FLAKES ARE JUST FOR MASHED POTATOES, think again! In this recipe, they make a delicious breading for shrimp. Try them with my warm pineapple salsa, and you won't want them with anything else!

---

1 POUND SHRIMP, PEELED AND DEVEINED

KOSHER SALT

1 LARGE EGG BEATEN WITH 1 TABLESPOON

WATER TO MAKE EGG WASH

1/2 CUP INSTANT POTATO FLAKES

COOKING SPRAY

CHILE POWDER, FOR GARNISH

WARM PINEAPPLE SALSA, FOR SERVING

1. Season shrimp with salt, then dip in egg wash, then in potato flakes, coating both sides well.

2. Set the air fryer to 400°F. Working in batches, spray shrimp on all sides and place in the air fryer basket, making sure they don't overlap. Cook until golden brown and crispy, 5–6 minutes.

3. To serve, place shrimp on serving plate, drizzle with Warm Pineapple Salsa, and garnish with a sprinkling of chile powder.

Try it with...

WARM PINEAPPLE SALSA

2 TABLESPOONS CANOLA OIL

1 RED ONION, DICED

KOSHER SALT

1/3 PINEAPPLE, DICED

1/2 JALAPEÑO PEPPER, DICED WITH SEEDS

1/2 CUP DARK RUM

2 KUMQUATS, THINLY SLICED; OR, 2 CLEMENTINES, PEELED AND SLICED AND THE ZEST 1/2 LEMON

2 TABLESPOONS SUGAR (PREFERABLY TURBINADO)

2 TABLESPOONS SOY SAUCE (PREFERABLY NATURALLY BREWED)

In a medium sauté pan over medium-high heat, heat oil, then add onions, and season with salt to taste. Sauté about 2 minutes to soften onion. Add pineapple and jalapeño and cook until softened, another 2 minutes. Carefully add rum (it may flame!) and flambée until rum cooks off. Add kumquats, sugar, and soy sauce. Taste and adjust seasoning. Reserve and keep warm.

STUFFED *Shrimp*

THESE STUFFED SHRIMP ARE SO TASTY you'll be dreaming about them later. Use the biggest shrimp you can find and butterfly them by cutting along their back from the thickest end to the thinnest. Pack them with bread crumbs and seasonings and you're off to the air fryer!

1 CUP PANKO (JAPANESE BREAD CRUMBS)

5 CLOVES GARLIC

1 CUP PACKED PARSLEY LEAVES

KOSHER SALT

3 TABLESPOONS EXTRA-VIRGIN OLIVE OIL

8 COLOSSAL SHRIMP, BUTTERFLIED

COOKING SPRAY

1. In a food processor, blend panko, garlic, and parsley with pinch of salt and drizzle in extra-virgin olive oil. Stuff shrimp with the mixture.

2. Set the air fryer to 375°F. Carefully spray the outside of the shrimp and place in a single layer in the air fryer basket. Cook for 8 to 10 minutes.

BACON-WRAPPED SHRIMP *with Pineapple*

BELIEVE IT OR NOT, bacon, shrimp, and pineapple are three flavors that complement each other beautifully—but even if you don't believe me, you probably know that your family is guaranteed to eat anything wrapped in bacon. Try this recipe with my sweet and smoky Carrot and Chipotle Syrup, which really takes this dish to the next level.

12 SLICES BACON

12 JUMBO SHRIMP, PEELED AND DEVEINED

1 SMALL PINEAPPLE, PEELED, CORED, AND CUT INTO 1-INCH DICE

KOSHER SALT AND FRESHLY GROUND BLACK PEPPER

6 CUPS COOKED JASMINE RICE

1/4 CUP CARROT-CHIPOTLE SYRUP (OPTIONAL)

2 TABLESPOONS CHOPPED CHIVES (OPTIONAL)

1. Lay bacon on a clean work surface. Place shrimp on each slice toward the top. Curl each shrimp around a pineapple chunk, then roll it tightly in bacon. Season lightly with salt and pepper.

2. Set the air fryer to 375ºF. Working in batches, lay each wrapped shrimp flat in a single layer in the air fryer basket and cook, until the bacon is brown and crispy and the shrimp are cooked through, 8 to 10 minutes. Serve over rice and with Carrot-Chipotle Syrup, if desired.

Try it with...

CARROT-CHIPOTLE SYRUP

2 QUARTS FRESH CARROT JUICE

1 TEASPOON CHOPPED CANNED CHIPOTLE IN ADOBO

3/4 CUP GRAPESEED OIL

KOSHER SALT AND FRESHLY GROUND BLACK PEPPER

In a large nonreactive saucepan, bring carrot juice to a gentle simmer over low heat. Reduce juice until all the liquid is evaporated, leaving a wet residue, about 45 minutes. With a heat-resistant rubber spatula, scrape the residue from the pan and transfer it to a blender. Add chipotle, and blend at high speed. With the machine running, drizzle in oil, very slowly at first, until the mixture is emulsified; then add the oil more quickly to prevent the sauce from breaking. Season with salt and pepper. Use or store in an airtight container in the refrigerator for up to 2 weeks. Makes about 1 cup.

SHRIMP *with Spicy Cucumber Sambal*

IN ADDITION TO BEING THE NAME OF A CHILE PASTE, sambal is a spicy Asian vegetable relish. It goes great with chicken, beef, or any other meat, really. But here I've paired it with shrimp and topped it off with a tangy mixture of Greek yogurt and lemon zest. Together, they make a palate-pleasing combo that makes for a memorable dinner during the hot summer months. Enjoy!

---

1 SMALL CUCUMBER, WITH SOME PEEL LEFT ON, SEEDED, AND FINELY DICED

1 TEASPOON GRANULATED SUGAR

KOSHER SALT

JUICE OF 2 LEMONS

JUICE OF 4 LIMES

1 SHALLOT, FINELY DICED

1/2 SERRANO PEPPER OR 2 FRESH THAI BIRD CHILES, QUARTERED AND SLICED THIN

2 LARGE CLOVES GARLIC, MINCED

1 TABLESPOON SAMBAL (CHILE PASTE) OR SRIRACHA SAUCE

1 KNOB GINGER, PEELED AND GRATED

1 TABLESPOON WHITE PEPPER, PLUS ADDITIONAL FOR SEASONING

1/2 CUP MINCED CILANTRO LEAVES

1/2 CUP GREEK YOGURT OR CREME FRAÎCHE

ZEST OF 1 LEMON

12 LARGE SHRIMP, PEELED AND DEVEINED

COOKING SPRAY

1. In a medium bowl, add cucumber and sugar, and season to taste with salt. Mix in citrus juices, shallot, chiles, garlic, sambal, ginger, 1 tablespoon white pepper, and cilantro. Set aside to rest.

2. In a separate bowl, whisk Greek yogurt until smooth. Season with salt and white pepper to taste and stir in lemon zest.

3. Season shrimp with salt and white pepper and spray on all sides with cooking spray.

4. Set the air fryer to 400°F. Working in batches if necessary, place shrimp in the air fryer basket without overlapping. Cook for 8 to 10 minutes, flipping once during the cook time.

5. To serve, place a dollop of Greek yogurt on the bottom of 4 plates (or on a platter) and top each with 3 pieces of shrimp. Top with cucumber sambal.

Scallion-Crusted COD

ONE OF MY FAVORITE FISH, cod has a delicious sweet, yet mild taste and a divine flaky texture. That natural sweetness is perfectly accented by the mango salsa I've included here, which also has quite a bit of heat! I've included a recipe to make more than you need for the cod, so make sure to buy a bag of chips to go with it.

---

4 (6- TO 8-OUNCE) SKINLESS COD FILLETS, PREFERABLY CENTER-CUT

KOSHER SALT AND FRESHLY GROUND BLACK PEPPER

2 CUPS PANKO (JAPANESE BREAD CRUMBS), OR REGULAR BREAD CRUMBS

1/2 CUP THINLY SLICED SCALLIONS

1 EGG BEATEN WITH 1 TABLESPOON WATER FOR EGG WASH

2 TABLESPOONS GRAPESEED OR CANOLA OIL

1/4 CUP CHOPPED FRESH CILANTRO

1. Season cod on both sides with salt and pepper. On a large plate, combine panko and scallions. Using a pastry brush, lightly brush fillets with egg wash and dredge in panko on both sides.

2. Set the air fryer to 375ºF. Working in batches, place 2 fillets in the air fryer basket. Cook for 4 to 6 minutes, or until cooked through, flipping once during the cook time.

3. Garnish with cilantro and serve with Spicy Mango Salsa, if desired.

Try it with...

SPICY MANGO SALSA

5 LARGE, RIPE MANGOS, PEELED AND DICED

2 MEDIUM RED ONIONS, DICED

2 RED JALAPEÑOS, STEMMED AND MINCED

1 TABLESPOON MINCED FRESH GINGER

2 TABLESPOONS SAMBAL (CHILE PASTE), OR HOT PEPPER SAUCE

1/3 CUP FRESH LIME JUICE (ABOUT 4 TO 8 LIMES)

KOSHER SALT AND FRESHLY GROUND BLACK PEPPER

In a large, nonreactive bowl, combine mangos, onions, jalapeños, ginger, sambal, and lime juice, and blend gently. Season with salt and pepper. Use or refrigerate up to 1½ weeks.

Crispy FISH FILLET

I LOVE A GOOD FISH FILLET, and when they're made in the air fryer, they turn out so perfectly you'll never want to visit the drive-thru for one again.

---

4 (4-OUNCE) FISH FILLETS, DEBONED AND SKINLESS

KOSHER SALT AND FRESHLY GROUND BLACK PEPPER

2 CUPS PANKO (JAPANESE BREAD CRUMBS)

1 TABLESPOON DRIED THYME

1 TABLESPOON DRIED BASIL

1 TEASPOON COARSELY GROUND BLACK PEPPER

1 TEASPOON CHILE POWDER

2 CUPS ALL-PURPOSE FLOUR

3 LARGE EGGS, WHISKED WITH 1 TABLESPOON WATER

COOKING SPRAY

---

1. Season fish with salt and pepper. Combine panko, thyme, basil, pepper, and chile powder in a shallow dish. Place flour and egg mixture in 2 separate shallow dishes. Lightly coat each fillet in flour, then eggs, then bread crumbs, removing excess after each dipping.

2. Set the air fryer to 375°F. Working in batches, spray fish fillets on all sides with cooking spray and place 2 fillets in the air fryer basket. Cook for 8 to 10 minutes, or until cooked through, flipping once during the cook time.

3. Serve with Spicy Mango Salsa (page 93) or Warm Pineapple Salsa (page 86).

TERIYAKI SALMON
with Lime Rice

SALMON IS ONE OF THE BEST SHOWCASES for the sweet tartness of teriyaki glaze, and it goes perfectly with the gently acidic lime rice I've paired it with in this dish.

---

1 CUP TERIYAKI SAUCE, PLUS EXTRA FOR GARNISH

4 (6- TO 8-OUNCE) SKIN-ON SALMON FILLETS, PREFERABLY CENTER-CUT

KOSHER SALT AND FRESHLY GROUND BLACK PEPPER

2 CUPS COOKED RICE, PREFERABLY SUSHI RICE

JUICE OF 3 LIMES

2 TABLESPOONS MINCED FRESH CHIVES OR GREEN PARTS OF SCALLIONS

2 TEASPOONS SESAME SEEDS

1. Place salmon in resealable plastic bag with teriyaki sauce and marinate for 30 minutes. After removing, brush off excess sauce and lightly season with salt and pepper.

2. Set the air fryer to 375ºF. Working in batches, place 2 salmon fillets in the air fryer basket. Cook for 10 minutes. Repeat with remaining fillets.

3. Meanwhile, in a medium bowl, combine hot rice with lime juice and chives, and mix gently. Mound some rice on each plate. Brush salmon with some of the remaining teriyaki sauce and sprinkle with sesame seeds before placing on top of the rice for serving.

BOURBON-GLAZED SALMON *with Roasted Asparagus*

THE BOURBON IN THIS SALMON GLAZE MAKES IT SWEET YET SMOKY. Cook the asparagus under the salmon and it will soak up all that delicious flavor, too!

3 TABLESPOONS BOURBON

1/3 CUP LOW-SODIUM SOY SAUCE (PREFERABLY NATURALLY BREWED)

1 TEASPOON LIME JUICE

1 TEASPOON SESAME OIL

1 TEASPOON GRATED GINGER

1 TEASPOON MINCED GARLIC

3 TABLESPOONS HONEY

2 (5-OUNCE) SALMON FILLETS

1 BUNCH FRESH ASPARAGUS

1. In a bowl, mix together bourbon, soy sauce, lime juice, sesame oil, ginger, garlic, and honey until smooth and incorporated. Pour mixture over salmon, cover, and place in the refrigerator. Let marinate for 30 minutes.

2. Meanwhile, cut asparagus to fit basket. Set the air fryer to 375ºF. Add asparagus to the bottom of the air fryer basket, then remove salmon from glaze and lay on top of asparagus. Cook for 10 minutes (longer for larger pieces of salmon); serve immediately.

Potato-Chip Crusted SALMON

POTATO CHIPS GIVE THIS FISH ITS IRRESISTIBLE CRUNCHINESS—I like to call it "fish and chips" although it's not the kind most people are expecting!

1 CUP ALL-PURPOSE FLOUR

3 LARGE EGGS, BEATEN

3 CUPS KETTLE-COOKED POTATO CHIPS (LIKE CAPE COD ORIGINAL), CRUSHED

1/2 TEASPOON PAPRIKA

3/4 TEASPOON CHILI POWDER

KOSHER SALT AND FRESHLY GROUND BLACK PEPPER

4 (4-OUNCE) SKINLESS WILD SALMON FILLETS

COOKING SPRAY

1. Place flour, eggs, and potato chips in three shallow dishes. Mix paprika and chili powder into the chip pieces.

2. Very lightly salt fish. Dredge fish fillets first in flour, then egg, then seasoned potato chips, shaking off excess each time. (Use a pair of tongs to prevent breaded hands.) Spray on all sides with cooking spray.

3. Set the air fryer to 400ºF. Working in batches, place 2 salmon fillets in the air fryer basket. Cook for 12 minutes, longer for larger fillets. Repeat with the remaining fillets. Serve with Mango Salsa (page 93).

FLASHED SALMON
with Wasabi and Avocado

IF YOU CAN'T TELL, I LOVE SALMON, and nowhere is it more decadent than thinly sliced and paired with avocado and wasabi. If you've ever had sushi, you're probably familiar with the spicy green stuff (wasabi) that comes on the side. If you can't find wasabi paste in the Asian section of your grocery store, just save some the next time you get sushi and try it in this impressive recipe.

---

1 TABLESPOON FRESH LEMON JUICE

1 LEVEL TABLESPOON WASABI PASTE

2 RIPE AVOCADOS, SLICED 1/2-INCH THICK

1 POUND SKINLESS CENTER-CUT SALMON FILLETS, SLICED VERY THINLY, SASHIMI-STYLE

1 TEASPOON SESAME OIL

MALDON SEA SALT, OR OTHER FLAKY SEA SALT

FRESHLY GROUND BLACK PEPPER

1. In a small bowl, combine lemon juice and wasabi and stir to mix. Slice avocado into ovenproof dishes (ramekins are perfect) and season with salt and black pepper. Brush lemon-wasabi mixture over avocado. Top with salmon slices, and lightly brush on sesame oil and season with salt and pepper.

2. Set the air fryer to 350ºF, and place ramekins in the air fryer basket. Cook for 5–10 minutes, depending on how thinly you sliced the salmon and desired level of doneness. Carefully remove hot dishes from the air fryer, and serve immediately.

POTATO-CRUSTED *Fish*

THIS EASY RECIPE MAKES THE PERFECT AIR-FRIED FISH and may become your go-to when you're in the mood for seafood.

---

4 SKINLESS FISH
FILLETS, SUCH AS TROUT
OR WHITEFISH

KOSHER SALT AND
FRESHLY GROUND
BLACK PEPPER

1/4 CUP DIJON MUSTARD
OR REHYDRATED CHINESE
MUSTARD

1 TABLESPOON SUGAR

2 CUPS INSTANT
POTATO FLAKES

COOKING SPRAY

1. Season fish with salt and pepper. In a bowl, combine mustard and sugar and brush on both sides of each fillet. Place potato flakes in shallow dish and season with salt. Press both sides of each fillet into potato flakes.

2. Set the air fryer to 375ºF. Working in batches, spray fish on all sides with cooking spray and place in the air fryer basket. Cook until fish is crispy and cooked through, 5 to 8 minutes. Remove to serving plate and repeat with remaining fillets. Serve with a side of greens.

Crispy Dijon TROUT

THIS RECIPE USES MUSTARD IN A DIFFERENT WAY, by combining it with the breading (and some scallions) before brushing it on. If you love Dijon mustard, you'll love this fish!

1/4 CUP DIJON MUSTARD

1 CUP PANKO (JAPANESE BREAD CRUMBS)

2 TABLESPOONS OLIVE OIL

3 SCALLIONS, SLICED THINLY, WHITE AND GREEN PARTS SEPARATED

4 SKINLESS RAINBOW TROUT FILLETS

KOSHER SALT AND FRESHLY GROUND BLACK PEPPER

COOKING SPRAY

LEMON, FOR SERVING

1. In a bowl, combine mustard with panko, olive oil, and scallion whites. Season trout with salt and pepper and place on prepared plate. Spread seasoned panko mixture over trout. Spray with cooking spray.

2. Set the air fryer to 375°F. Working in batches, carefully transfer 2 trout fillets to the air fryer basket. Cook for 5 to 8 minutes, then repeat with remaining fish fillets. Serve with lemon wedge for spritzing.

Air-Fried PORK CHOPS

IF YOU LOVE PORK CHOPS, try this easy version, perfect topped with gravy (for country-fried chops!) or my Warm Pineapple Salsa from page 86.

---

4 PORK CHOPS, CUT INTO 1/2-INCH THICK PIECES

KOSHER SALT AND FRESHLY GROUND BLACK PEPPER

3 LARGE EGGS, BEATEN

1/4 CUP 2% MILK

1 CUP ALL-PURPOSE FLOUR

COOKING SPRAY

1 CUP GRAVY

1. Season meat on both sides with salt and pepper. In large shallow bowl, whisk together eggs and milk. In separate shallow bowl, add flour.

2. Working with one piece at a time, dredge pork in flour. Turn to coat, shaking off excess. Place meat in egg mixture, turning to coat, then dredge again in flour. Repeat with remaining chops.

3. Set air fryer to 400°F. Working in batches, spray with cooking oil on all sides and then place in one layer in air fryer basket. Cook for 10 minutes, turning once during cook time.

CHORIZO-STUFFED
Pork Chops

WHAT'S BETTER THAN PORK? More pork! These pork chops are stuffed with spicy Mexican sausage, a.k.a. chorizo, for twice the yummy pork flavor.

4 BONE-IN PORK CHOPS, ABOUT 1 1/2 INCHES THICK

KOSHER SALT AND FRESHLY GROUND BLACK PEPPER

1 POUND GROUND CHORIZO OR OTHER SPICY SAUSAGE

COOKING SPRAY

1. Slice into pork chops from the side until the knife hits bone. Season with salt and pepper. Form chorizo into 4 patties and stuff into pork chops. Close pork chops with toothpicks. Spray on all sides with cooking spray.

2. Set the air fryer to 375ºF. Working in batches, place 2 pork chops in the air fryer basket and cook until cooked through, about 15 to 18 minutes. Transfer to cutting board and let sit for several minutes. Remove toothpicks before serving.

Korean PORK BELLY

PORK BELLY IS ONE OF THE MOST DELICIOUS PARTS OF THE PIG (it's where bacon comes from, if that tells you anything)! If you ever manage to get your hands on one (try a specialty market, Asian grocery store, or direct from a farm or butcher), here's how to do it right!

---

2 TABLESPOONS KOCHU KARU (KOREAN CHILE POWDER) OR CHIPOTLE CHILE POWDER

2 TABLESPOONS SUGAR

1 TABLESPOON KOSHER SALT

2 POUNDS PORK BELLY

COOKING SPRAY

1. In a small bowl, combine chile powder, sugar, and salt. Rub chile mixture all over pork belly, especially on the top fat. Place in refrigerator, uncovered, overnight.

2. The next day remove pork belly from refrigerator and score fat on top in a diamond pattern.

3. Set the air fryer to 300ºF. Place pork belly in the air fryer basket, and cook for 45 minutes. Drain fat from air fryer, turn up to 325ºF, and cook for another 45 minutes.

4. Let pork belly rest for a few minutes before slicing.

DIJON-SOY *Flank Steak*

HERE'S ANOTHER GREAT RECIPE incorporating the flavors of soy sauce and Dijon mustard. This time, they make up a marinade that brings out the deep notes in flank steak.

1/4 CUP SOY SAUCE

1 TABLESPOON SUGAR

1 TABLESPOON DIJON MUSTARD

1 TABLESPOON SESAME OIL

1/4 CUP CANOLA OIL

KOSHER SALT AND FRESHLY GROUND BLACK PEPPER

2 POUNDS FLANK STEAK, TRIMMED

1. In a large bowl, mix together soy sauce, sugar, and mustard, and whisk in oils. Season with salt and pepper. Rub into the steak and marinate for at least 2 hours and up to 24 hours.

2. Set the air fryer to 400°F. Working in batches, remove steak from marinade and place in a single layer in the air fryer basket. Cook for 5 minutes per side for medium rare. Let rest 5 minutes before slicing against the grain. Garnish with Chimichurri Sauce.

Try it with...

CHIMICHURRI SAUCE

1 CUP CHOPPED PARSLEY

4 CLOVES GARLIC

3/4 TEASPOON DRIED OREGANO

1/2 TEASPOON RED PEPPER FLAKES

1 TEASPOON KOSHER SALT

3/4 TEASPOON FRESHLY GROUND PEPPER

3/4 CUP VEGETABLE OR OLIVE OIL

2 TABLESPOONS RED WINE VINEGAR

2 TABLESPOONS LEMON JUICE

Place all ingredients in a blender or food processor and blend until puréed.

Fried MEATBALLS

MEATBALLS ARE SO POPULAR AROUND THE WORLD that just about every culture's cuisine has a version! Which isn't surprising, because it's only natural to form ground meat into a ball. These meatballs are not only fun to make, they're a delicious accompaniment to pasta, rice, or even on their own.

---

1 POUND GROUND SIRLOIN BEEF

1 LARGE EGG, BEATEN

1/4 CUP PANKO (JAPANESE BREAD CRUMBS)

1 TEASPOON DRIED PARSLEY (OR 1 TABLESPOON FRESH)

1 GARLIC CLOVE, MINCED

1/2 TEASPOON ONION POWDER

1 TEASPOON KOSHER SALT

1/4 TEASPOON FRESHLY GROUND BLACK PEPPER

COOKING SPRAY

1. In a large bowl, loosely mix all ingredients except cooking spray together with your hands.

2. Scoop approximately 3 tablespoons of the mixture into the palm of your hand and roll into a ball. Repeat with remaining mixture.

3. Spray meatballs on all sides with cooking spray and place in the air fryer basket, leaving room between each meatball. You may need to work in batches.

4. Set air fryer to 400ºF. Cook until cooked through and golden, about 12 minutes. Repeat with remaining meatballs if necessary.

ASIAN *Hamburger Pockets*

AS A KID SPENDING SUMMERS WITH MY GRANDPARENTS, I knew these savory pockets of ground beef as shiar-bing, a treat we'd often have for dim sum, or Taiwanese brunch. This slightly less authentic version still has the pop of flavor of the original, with much less work.

---

1 TABLESPOON CANOLA OIL

1 POUND GROUND BEEF

1 POUND GROUND PORK

1 CUP SLICED SCALLIONS, WHITE AND GREEN PARTS

1 TABLESPOON MINCED FRESH GINGER

2 TABLESPOONS SOY SAUCE (PREFERABLY NATURALLY BREWED)

1 TEASPOON COARSELY GROUND BLACK PEPPER

1 POUND BLUE GINGER CRACKER DOUGH (PAGE 24) OR 2 REFRIGERATED PIE CRUSTS

COOKING SPRAY

1. Heat oil in a large skillet over medium-high heat. Add beef and pork and cook, stirring and breaking up occasionally, until browned, about 8 minutes. Drain fat.

2. Add scallions, ginger, soy sauce, and pepper and mix lightly. Set aside until completely cooled.

3. Divide the dough into 4 equal pieces and shape each into a rough ball. Flour a work surface, and roll each piece of dough into 14-inch rounds. Place a quarter of the meat mixture in the center of each dough, bring up the sides, and twist into a spiral to seal. Slightly flatten the dough-enclosed "burgers." Spray on all sides with cooking spray.

4. Set the air fryer to 350ºF. Working in batches, place burgers in the air fryer basket seam-side down. Cook for 10 to 12 minutes, or until golden. Remove to serving plate and repeat with remaining burgers. Allow the pockets to rest for about 4 minutes. Halve and

Mini MEATLOAVES

GIVE EACH PERSON IN YOUR FAMILY THEIR OWN PERSONAL MEATLOAF with this fun (and delicious!) recipe and don't be surprised if you're hailed as a dinner hero.

1/2 POUND GROUND SIRLOIN BEEF

1/2 POUND GROUND TURKEY OR CHICKEN

1/2 CUP PANKO (JAPANESE BREAD CRUMBS)

1/4 CUP MUSHROOMS, MINCED (PREFERABLY PORTABELLO CAPS)

1 LARGE EGG, SLIGHTLY BEATEN

2 TEASPOONS WORCESTERSHIRE SAUCE

2 GARLIC CLOVES, MINCED

1 SCALLION, CHOPPED

2 TEASPOONS GROUND CUMIN

1 TEASPOON DRIED THYME

1 TEASPOON SALT

1/2 TEASPOON FRESHLY GROUND BLACK PEPPER

1/8 TEASPOON CAYENNE PEPPER

1/4 CUP KETCHUP

1. In a large bowl, combine ground sirloin, ground turkey or chicken, panko, mushrooms, egg, Worcestershire sauce, garlic, scallion, cumin, thyme, salt, pepper, and cayenne pepper. Form into 4 loaves.

2. Set air fryer to 350ºF. Working in batches, place 2 loaves at a time in air fryer basket. Cover each with 1 tablespoon ketchup. Cook until cooked through, 15–20 minutes. Repeat with remaining loaves.

Beef STIR-FRY STRIPS

MAKE STIR-FRY EVEN EASIER with this air-fried version. You can even roast vegetables right alongside these deliciously seasoned beef strips by simply spraying some fresh veggies with cooking spray and placing them on top while the beef is cooking. Enjoy!

1/2 CUP EXTRA-VIRGIN OLIVE OIL

1 TABLESPOON MINCED GARLIC

1 TABLESPOON MINCED GINGER

1 TEASPOON DRIED TARRAGON

1 TEASPOON DRIED PARSLEY

1 TABLESPOON CHOPPED FRESH ROSEMARY

1 (1-POUND) BOTTOM ROUND BEEF

KOSHER SALT AND FRESHLY GROUND BLACK PEPPER

1 TEASPOON SESAME SEEDS

1. Combine olive oil, garlic, ginger, tarragon, parsley, and rosemary. Pour into resealable plastic bag.

2. On a clean work surface, cut bottom round into 1-inch strips. Add to bag and allow to marinate in the refrigerator at least 2 hours or overnight.

3. Set the air fryer to 400ºF. Remove strips from marinade and place in single layer in the air fryer basket. Cook for 6 to 8 minutes, or until cooked through. Remove from air fryer, allow to rest 5 minutes.

4. Sprinkle with sesame seeds and serve with sliced red peppers or other vegetables over rice.

ASIAN SPICED *Lamb Chops*

IF YOU HAVE SPRUNG FOR LAMB CHOPS, make them memorable with this Asian-inspired marinade that's also great for beef! If you prefer them less spicy, simply omit the chile powder.

1/4 CUP KUCHO JANG (KOREAN CHILE PASTE) OR CHILE POWDER

1/4 CUP DIJON MUSTARD

3 TABLESPOONS MINCED FRESH GINGER

3 TABLESPOONS MINCED GARLIC

1/4 CUP CANOLA OIL

1/4 CUP SOY SAUCE OR TAMARI

FRESHLY GROUND BLACK PEPPER

4 LAMB CHOPS

1. In a large bowl, whisk together chile powder, Dijon mustard, ginger, garlic, canola oil, soy sauce, and pepper. Add lamb chops, cover with plastic wrap, and refrigerate at least 2 hours or overnight.

2. Set the air fryer to 375°F. Working in batches, place lamb chops in the air fryer basket in a single layer. Cook for 20 to 25 minutes, or until cooked through. Transfer to cutting board and let rest for 5 minutes. Serve with rice pilaf and a drizzle of pesto sauce.

EGGS *Florentine*

EGGS FLORENTINE IS A BREAKFAST DISH that's fancy enough for dinner. Serve with a piece of crusty bread or next to a grilled cheese sandwich!

1 TABLESPOON BUTTER, MELTED

1/2 CUP FRESH SPINACH

2 EGGS

2 TABLESPOONS SHREDDED PARMESAN CHEESE

KOSHER SALT AND FRESHLY GROUND PEPPER

6 GRAPE TOMATOES, HALVED

1. Brush the inside of a heat-safe container, like a mini pie tin or oversized oven-safe ramekin, with melted butter. Add spinach evenly across the bottom and add cracked eggs on top. Season with salt and pepper to taste; sprinkle with Parmesan.

2. Set the air fryer to 325ºF and place the dish in the air fryer basket. Cook for 8 minutes for soft-cooked and 10 minutes for hard-cooked eggs. When finished, top with tomatoes and serve immediately.

Crispy Breaded EGGPLANT

EGGPLANT IS SO MEATY AND FLAVORFUL, you can eat it for dinner and not even realize it's vegetarian! This crispy, breaded version also packs a bit of a spicy kick.

3 JAPANESE EGGPLANT, HALVED LENGTHWISE AND FLESH SCORED DIAGONALLY

KOSHER SALT AND FRESHLY GROUND BLACK PEPPER

COOKING SPRAY

1 TABLESPOON SESAME OIL

3 TABLESPOONS CANOLA OIL

2 TABLESPOONS SRIRACHA SAUCE

1 CUP PANKO (JAPANESE BREAD CRUMBS)

EXTRA-VIRGIN OLIVE OIL, FOR DRIZZLING

1. Season eggplant with salt and pepper and spray all over with cooking spray. In a small bowl, mix together sesame oil, canola oil, and Sriracha. Brush mixture onto sliced side of eggplant and dip into panko. Moisten bread crumbs on top with a drizzle of olive oil.

2. Set the air fryer to 400°F. Working in batches if necessary, place eggplant bread crumb–side up in a single layer in the air fryer basket. Cook until golden brown and delicious (GB&D), 8 to 10 minutes. To serve, plate with a few tablespoons Chile Yogurt spooned over hot eggplant.

Try it with...

CHILE YOGURT

1 CUP NONFAT GREEK YOGURT

3 SCALLIONS, THINLY SLICED

1 LARGE TOMATO, SEEDED AND DICED

8 LEAVES THAI BASIL (OR REGULAR BASIL), THINLY SLICED

1 TABLESPOON SRIRACHA SAUCE

KOSHER SALT AND FRESHLY GROUND BLACK PEPPER

In a bowl, combine Greek yogurt, scallions, tomato, basil, and Sriracha sauce. Add salt and pepper to taste. Store leftovers in the refrigerator.

TANTALIZING SIDES

Air Fryer FRENCH FRIES

AIR FRYERS WERE PRACTICALLY INVENTED TO MAKE GREAT FRENCH FRIES! And you'll see why when you try them and never want to go through the drive-thru again. I used seasoned salt in this recipe but you can also just use regular kosher salt.

---

2 LARGE BAKING POTATOES, PEELED AND CUT EVENLY INTO 1/4-INCH FRIES

2 TABLESPOONS OLIVE OIL

1 TABLESPOON SEASONED SALT

1. Put raw fries in a bowl and cover with cool water. Drain and repeat with fresh water. Drain again, and place fries on paper towels to dry. Pat with another paper towel to blot dry.

2. Put dry French fries in a bowl and drizzle with olive oil, sprinkle with seasoned salt, and toss to coat.

3. Set air fryer to 325ºF. Add fries to the air fryer basket and cook for 7 minutes. Remove to a paper towel–lined plate.

4. Turn air fryer up to 400ºF degrees. Blot French fries dry again using paper towels. Return to the air fryer basket and cook for 5 minutes. Remove basket and shake the French fries; continue cooking for 2 to 5 additional minutes, depending on how dark and crispy you like your fries.

ROSEMARY *Potatoes*

ROASTED POTATOES WITH A BIT OF ROSEMARY ARE THE PERFECT SIDE DISH for ham, steak, and other hearty meats. Just the smell of rosemary, in fact, enhances any meal!

---

1 POUND SMALL RED POTATOES

1 TABLESPOON EXTRA-VIRGIN OLIVE OIL

1 TEASPOON KOSHER SALT

1/2 TEASPOON FRESHLY GROUND BLACK PEPPER

1 TABLESPOON FRESH ROSEMARY

1. Halve or quarter potatoes, depending on their size. You want each piece to be bite-sized.

2. In a large bowl, toss potato pieces with olive oil, salt, and pepper.

3. Set air fryer to 400ºF. Place potatoes in a single layer in the air fryer basket. Cook for 15 to 20 minutes, shaking basket every 4 to 5 minutes to stir potatoes. Toss with fresh rosemary before serving.

SWEET POTATO FRIES
with Chile Aioli

SWEET POTATO FRIES ARE NOT ONLY HEALTHIER THAN FRENCH FRIES, they have a crave-worthy taste that's all their own. Serve them with ketchup or try them with my Chile Aioli (a fancy name for Spicy Mayonnaise), which is the perfect accompaniment.

---

3 LARGE SWEET POTATOES, PEELED AND CUT EVENLY INTO 1/4-INCH FRIES

1 CUP CORNSTARCH

2 EGG YOLKS

1 HEAPING TEASPOON MINCED GARLIC

1/4 CUP CHILI OIL (PREFERABLY ONE WITH A SESAME-OIL BASE)

KOSHER SALT AND FRESHLY GROUND BLACK PEPPER TO TASTE

1. Soak raw fries in ice water for 5 to 10 minutes. Drain, and place fries on paper towels to dry. Pat with another paper towel to blot dry.

2. Set air fryer to 325ºF. Add fries to the air fryer basket and cook for 7 minutes, shaking the basket once during cooking time. Place cooked fries in the refrigerator to chill.

3. In a large bowl, mix cornstarch with enough water to make a slurry. Place chilled fries in a mesh strainer and dip into cornstarch slurry until fries are well coated.

4. Set air fryer to 400ºF. Working in batches, place fries in air fryer basket in a single layer and cook for 5 minutes. Remove basket and flip, and continue cooking until golden brown and delicious (GB&D), another 2 to 5 minutes.

Try it with...

CHILE AIOLI

2 TEASPOONS
MINCED GARLIC

2 EGG YOLKS

1/2 CUP PLUS
2 TABLESPOONS
GRAPESEED OIL

JUICE OF 1 LEMON

1 TABLESPOON SAMBAL
OR SRIRACHA SAUCE

2 TABLESPOONS
CHOPPED CHIVES

KOSHER SALT AND
FRESHLY GROUND
BLACK PEPPER

In a food processor, combine garlic and yolks and blend until smooth and yolks are pale and creamy. With food processor running, very slowly drizzle in oil. You want an emulsification to form, so go slowly; once about a quarter of the oil had been added, you can pour the rest in a steady stream. Add lemon juice and blend briefly. Stir in sambal and chives. Season with salt and pepper.

Chipotle-Soy Sweet Potato
HOME FRIES

HERE'S AN ORIGINAL TAKE ON SWEET POTATOES that balances their sweetness with the smoky flavor of chipotle chiles and the richness of soy sauce. You can find cans of chipotles in adobo sauce in the Mexican section of your grocery store.

---

1 POUND SWEET POTATOES, PEELED AND CUT INTO 3/4-INCH DICE

1 ONION, 3/4-INCH DICE

KOSHER SALT AND FRESHLY GROUND BLACK PEPPER

2 TABLESPOONS CANOLA OIL, PLUS MORE FOR DRIZZLING

1/2 CUP LOW-SODIUM SOY SAUCE (PREFERABLY NATURALLY BREWED)

3 TABLESPOONS BROWN SUGAR

1 TABLESPOON CHOPPED CANNED CHIPOTLE IN ADOBO SAUCE

JUICE OF 2 LIMES

2 TABLESPOONS CHOPPED CHIVES OR GREEN PARTS OF SCALLIONS, FOR GARNISH

1. In a large bowl, toss sweet potatoes and onion with salt and pepper and oil to coat.

2. Set the air fryer to 350ºF. Place sweet poatoes in the air fryer basket and cook for 20 to 25 minutes, stirring or shaking the basket several times during cook time.

3. Meanwhile, in a small saucepan, add soy sauce, brown sugar, chipotle, and lime juice and cook until reduced by 75 percent. Transfer to a blender and blend on high speed, drizzling in oil until smooth. Drizzle over sweet potatoes and garnish with chives.

CARROTS *with Fennel*

FENNEL IS A NATURAL COMPLEMENT TO CARROTS. Add some ground fennel seed to this simple air fryer recipe and you won't mind eating your vegetables!

1 (16-OUNCE) BAG BABY CARROTS

1 TEASPOON GROUND FENNEL SEED

KOSHER SALT AND FRESHLY GROUND BLACK PEPPER

1. In a bowl, combine carrots, fennel seed, salt, and pepper to taste.

2. Set the air fryer to 375°F. Place carrots in the air fryer basket and cook for 12 to 15 minutes.

SEASONED *Cauliflower Steaks*

CAULIFLOWER IS HAVING ITS MOMENT IN THE SUN as the vegetable *du jour,* and it deserves it! Air frying really brings out its flavor, so don't be surprised if these cauliflower steaks steal the show from your main dish.

---

1 HEAD CAULIFLOWER

2 TABLESPOONS DIJON MUSTARD

2 TABLESPOONS HOISIN SAUCE

KOSHER SALT AND FRESHLY GROUND BLACK PEPPER

1/2 TEASPOON SESAME OIL, FOR SERVING

2 TABLESPOONS SLICED SCALLION GREENS, FOR GARNISH

1. With a sharp knife, core the cauliflower. Cut two "steaks" by cutting large slices from center of cauliflower, about 1-inch thick.

2. Brush both sides of each "steak" with mustard and hoisin. Season with salt and pepper.

3. Set the air fryer to 400ºF. Working in batches, lay the cauliflower flat in a single layer the air fryer basket. Cook for about 20 minutes. Repeat with remaining cauliflower.

4. Drizzle cauliflower steaks with sesame oil and top with scallion greens and serve.

Creamy Twice-Fried
POTATOES

YOU'LL LOVE THE CREAMY FILLING in these twice-fried (rather than "twice-baked") potatoes. Add some crumbled bacon for an even bigger treat!

2 LARGE BAKING POTATOES

CANOLA OIL

1/2 BUNCH SCALLIONS, THINLY SLICED, WHITE AND GREEN PARTS SEPARATED

1 CUP HEAVY CREAM

1 1/2 TABLESPOONS DIJON MUSTARD OR REHYDRATED CHINESE MUSTARD

KOSHER SALT AND FRESHLY GROUND BLACK PEPPER

2 TABLESPOONS BUTTER

1. Set air fryer to 350ºF. Add potatoes to air fryer basket, and cook until a knife can easily be inserted into their centers, about 25 to 35 minutes, turning halfway through cooking time. Remove and allow to cool slightly.

2. Meanwhile, in a saucepan over medium heat, add oil to coat and sauté scallion whites for about 30 seconds. Add cream and reduce by 25 percent, stirring occasionally. Whisk in mustard and season with salt and pepper.

3. Once potatoes are cool enough to handle, scoop out potato flesh, saving the shells. In a large bowl, combine potato flesh, cream mixture, and butter. Season and check for flavor. Stuff reserved potato skins with potato mixture.

4. Set the air fryer to 375ºF. Working in batches, place stuffed potatoes in the air fryer basket. Cook until warmed though, about 5 minutes.

BACON *Brussels Sprouts*

BRUSSELS SPROUTS GET A BAD RAP, but they're actually a flavorful green that kids usually love—especially if they're made with bacon.

---

4 SLICES THICKLY SLICED BACON

1 POUND BRUSSELS SPROUTS, QUARTERED

1 TABLESPOON EXTRA

VIRGIN OLIVE OIL

1 SMALL ONION, THINLY SLICED

1/2 TEASPOON KOCHU KARU OR CHILE POWDER

1/2 TEASPOON KOSHER SALT

1/4 TEASPOON FRESHLY GROUND BLACK PEPPER

1. Set air fryer to 350ºF. Add bacon slices to air fryer basket and cook until crispy, about 8 minutes. Remove to a paper towel-lined plate and set aside. Drain fat from air fryer.

2. Toss Brussels sprouts with olive oil, onion, chile powder, salt, and pepper.

3. Set the air fryer to 375ºF and place Brussels sprouts in the air fryer basket. Cook until Brussels sprouts are tender, 15 to 18 minutes, shaking once or twice during cook time.

4. In a serving bowl, crumble bacon slices and toss with Brussels sprouts.

MACARONI *and* CHEESE

WHETHER YOU'RE LOOKING FOR COMFORT FOOD on a cold winter's day or an enjoyable snack on a sunny afternoon, Mac and Cheese always fits the bill. This take on it features three different cheese and of course, is easy as pie (even easier, actually!) in the air fryer.

1 CUP COOKED PASTA SHELLS

1/2 CUP HEAVY CREAM

1/4 CUP SHREDDED CHEDDAR CHEESE

1/4 CUP SHREDDED SWISS CHEESE

1 TABLESPOON MELTED BUTTER

1/4 CUP PANKO (JAPANESE BREAD CRUMBS)

1 TABLESPOON GRATED PARMESAN CHEESE

1. In an oven-safe bowl that fits in the air fryer (or several ramekins), combine pasta, cream, Cheddar, and Swiss cheese; stir well.

2. Set the air fryer to 325ºF. Place baking dish in the air fryer basket and cook for 8 minutes; stir.

3. Meanwhile, combine butter, panko, and parmesan cheese. Put Parmesan mixture on top of pasta, set air fryer to 350ºF, and cook until golden brown, 6 to 8 more minutes. Serve immediately.

DREAM-
WORTHY
DESSERTS

Air Fryer DOUGHNUTS

TAKE YOUR DOUGHNUTS FAR FROM THE EVERYDAY with this gourmet recipe I crafted with a secret ingredient: mashed potatoes. Use some of your leftovers, or make them the instant way...either way, you'll love the depth they add to this classic that's perfect for dessert, breakfast, or any time in between.

1/2 CUP MILK

1 (1/4-OUNCE) PACKET ACTIVE DRY YEAST

1/4 CUP WATER

1/4 CUP PLUS 2 TABLESPOONS CORN SYRUP

1 EGG

3 3/4 CUPS ALL-PURPOSE FLOUR

4 TABLESPOONS COLD UNSALTED BUTTER, CUT INTO 1-INCH CUBES

1/4 CUP MASHED POTATOES

1/2 TEASPOON SALT

COOKING SPRAY

1. In a standing mixer with the paddle attachment, combine milk and yeast. Add remaining ingredients in order, and, on low speed, mix until well incorporated, about 5 minutes. Increase speed to medium and work the dough a bit more, until it's shiny and very stretchy.

2. Place dough in a large, lightly greased bowl and let rise at room temperature, covered, until doubled in volume, about 1½ to 2 hours.

3. Turn out dough onto a lightly floured surface and knead until smooth. Roll out to ½-inch thick, cut into strips, then form into rounds. Let sit, covered with a towel, in a warm place for 30 minutes to let rise. (An oven with only the pilot light on is a good place.)

4. Set the air fryer to 400ºF. Spray both sides of the dough with cooking spray, and working in batches, place in a single layer in the air fryer basket. Cook until golden, about 5 minutes, flipping halfway through cooking time.

DOUGHNUT HOLES
with Ginger Whipped Cream

HERE'S ANOTHER GREAT RECIPE you can make with my doughnut dough (page 139). Or, if you're looking for something even quicker, simply use some store-bought crescent roll dough instead!

1/2 POUND MASTER DOUGHNUT DOUGH (PAGE 139), OR REFRIGERATED CRESCENT ROLL DOUGH

COOKING SPRAY

1 TABLESPOON FIVE-SPICE POWDER

1/2 CUP SUGAR

1 CUP WHIPPED CREAM

1. On a floured work surface, roll out dough to ½-inch thick. Cut dough into 1-inch rounds and place on a parchment-lined or greased cookie sheet. If using Master Doughnut dough, let sit, covered with another sheet of parchment, in a warm place for 30 minutes to let rise. (An oven with only the pilot light on is a good place.)

2. Set the air fryer to 400ºF. Spray doughnut holes with cooking spray, and working in batches, place doughnuts in the air fryer basket, making sure to leave space between each one. Cook until golden brown and delicious (GB&D), about 5 minutes, flipping halfway through cooking time. Repeat with remaining doughnuts.

3. Meanwhile, in a small bowl, combine five-spice powder and sugar. Sprinkle finished doughnuts with spiced sugar. Serve hot donut holes with whipped cream and, if desired, dip them in ginger syrup.

Try it with...

GINGER SYRUP

2 CUPS SUGAR

2 CUPS WATER

2 CUPS FRESH GINGER,
CUT INTO $1/8$-INCH
SLICES (ABOUT 2
LARGE HANDS)

In a medium saucepan over high heat, combine sugar, ginger and water and bring to a boil. Reduce heat and simmer until syrupy and reduced by half. Syrup should hold a line of a plate. Strain ginger pieces out and reserve syrup.

Warm "Éclair" SUNDAE

WHEN IS A DOUGHNUT NOT A DOUGHNUT? When it's an éclair! This recipe adds nuts, fruit, ice cream, and (of course) chocolate sauce to turn regular doughnuts into a decadent dessert. Spring for the best-quality ice cream and chocolate you can find for a truly magnificent end to your meal!

1/2 POUND MASTER DOUGHNUT DOUGH (PAGE 139), OR REFRIGERATED CRESCENT ROLL DOUGH

COOKING SPRAY

1 PINT VANILLA ICE CREAM

1 CUP CHOCOLATE SAUCE OR GANACHE

1/2 CUP TOASTED PINE NUTS, FOR GARNISH

1 PINT RASPBERRIES, FOR GARNISH

POWDERED SUGAR, FOR GARNISH

1. On a floured work surface, roll out dough to ½-inch thick and cut into 4 x 1-inch rectangles and place on a parchment-lined or greased cookie sheet. If using Master Doughnut Dough, let sit, covered with another sheet of parchment, in a warm place for 30 minutes to let rise. (An oven with only the pilot light on is a good place.)

2. Set the air fryer to 400ºF. Spray doughnut-eclairs on both sides with cooking spray. and working in batches, place in a single layer in the air fryer basket, making sure to leave space between each one. Cook until golden brown and delicious (GB&D), about 5 minutes, flipping halfway through cooking time. Repeat with remaining doughnuts.

3. Split each doughnut-eclair lengthwise down the middle and fill with 3 small scoops of ice cream; drizzle chocolate sauce over and around the plate. Garnish with pine nuts, raspberries, and powdered sugar.

FRUIT *Pockets*

THESE FRUIT POCKETS COULDN'T BE EASIER TO MAKE, and they're versatile too—just use any fresh fruit you have on hand, like strawberries, raspberries, or bananas. Or, if fruit isn't in season, pick up a can of pie filling!

1 (16.3-OUNCE) PACKAGE REFRIGERATED BISCUIT DOUGH FOR FLAKY BISCUITS

FLOUR, FOR DUSTING

FRESH FRUIT OR CANNED FRUIT-PIE FILLING

POWDERED SUGAR, FOR DUSTING

COOKING SPRAY

1. Roll out biscuit rounds on a floured surface until they are about 7 inches in diameter. Add fruit filling to center, then wet your fingers and rub them along the outer edges of the biscuit round. Fold the round in half over the filling and press dampened edges to seal.

2. Line air fryer basket with parchment paper and set to 350ºF. Working in batches, spray all sides of fruit pocket with cooking spray and place in a single layer in air fryer basket. Cook until golden, about 10 minutes. Sprinkle with powdered sugar before serving.

MOLTEN *Chocolate Cake*

JUST ONE LOOK AT DELECTABLE, mouthwatering cake with a melted chocolate middle and you'll *have* to take a bite!

---

8 TABLESPOONS (1 STICK) UNSALTED BUTTER

2/3 CUP DARK CHOCOLATE CHIPS

2 EGGS

1/4 CUP SUPERFINE SUGAR

2 TABLESPOONS ALL-PURPOSE FLOUR, PLUS MORE FOR FLOURING RAMEKINS

PINCH BAKING SODA

PINCH SALT

POWDERED SUGAR, FOR DUSTING

1. In a medium bowl, heat chocolate chips and butter together in the microwave on medium (50%) power until melted, about 3–5 minutes, stirring every 30–60 seconds. Set aside to cool slightly.

2. In separate bowl, whisk eggs and sugar together until pale and frothy.

3. Pour melted chocolate mixture into egg mixture. Fold in flour, baking soda, and salt with a spatula until evenly combined.

4. Grease and flour 4 air fryer–safe ramekins, then fill about three-quarters full.

5. Set air fryer to 375ºF. Working in batches, place ramekins in the air fryer basket and bake for 10 minutes. Repeat with remaining ramekins.

6. Allow cake to cool in ramekins for 2 minutes. Carefully turn ramekins upside down onto serving plate, tapping the bottom with a butter knife to loosen edges. Cake should release from ramekin with little effort and center should appear dark and gooey. Dust with powdered sugar before serving.

Mini APPLE PIES

DURING FALL APPLE SEASON, I find my pantry is overflowing with apples. Whether you've just gotten back from apple picking or you have a big bag from the supermarket you want to use up, this dessert is for you! If you don't have any apples and you're still craving apple pie, you can even use a can of apple pie filling.

---

2 TABLESPOONS BUTTER

4 PIE APPLES SUCH AS GRANNY SMITH, BRAEBURN, CORTLAND, OR GOLDEN DELICIOUS, CHOPPED

1/4 CUP BROWN SUGAR

1/2 TEASPOON GROUND CINNAMON

1 TEASPOON LEMON JUICE

FLOUR, FOR DUSTING

1 (11-OUNCE) PACKAGE FROZEN PUFF PASTRY SHEETS, THAWED

2 EGGS, BEATEN

1. In medium skillet, melt butter over medium heat. Add chopped apples, brown sugar, and cinnamon and cook, stirring occasionally, until apples are soft, about 15 minutes. Stir in lemon juice.

2. On a floured surface (and working quickly so your pastry dough doesn't become too soft), roll out puff pastry dough and cut into 6 x 6-inch squares. Add 2 heaping tablespoons of apple filling to the middle and spread toward one corner of your square. Lift the opposite corner of dough and fold over filling; you want that corner to stay up in the air on top of the filling.

3. Line air fryer basket with parchment paper and set to 400°F. Working in batches, carefully move the turnovers into the air fryer basket in a single layer. Brush outsides of pastry with egg. Cook for 10 minutes. Remove, and repeat with any remaining turnovers. Serve warm with ice cream, if desired.

CAKE *Balls*

CAKE BALLS ARE AN IMMEDIATE PARTY PLEASER and are easier than you might think to make—you'll just need to find some "candy melts" in your baking aisle, which form the delicious outer coating of these instant-classic desserts.

---

1 (16-OUNCE) BOX
CAKE MIX

WATER, VEGETABLE OIL,
AND EGGS CALLED FOR
IN CAKE MIX PACKAGE
DIRECTIONS

3/4 CUP PREPARED
FROSTING

2 (10-OUNCE) PACKAGES
CANDY MELTS OR
ALMOND BARK

2 TABLESPOONS
VEGETABLE SHORTENING

1/2 CUP SPRINKLES

1. Set air fryer to 400ºF. In a large bowl, prepare cake mix according to package directions. Grease a 6-inch cake pan. Pour half of cake batter into pan and cook for 3 minutes. Then turn air fryer down to 325ºF and cook for 30 minutes more, or until toothpick inserted into the center comes out clean. Let cake rest for 5 minutes; then remove by inverting pan. Repeat with remaining cake batter.

2. In large bowl, crumble cake. Add frosting and mix well. Roll into balls about 1-inch thick and place on a parchment-lined cookie sheet. Freeze until firm, about 30 to 45 minutes.

3. In medium bowl, combine 1 package of candy melts and 1 tablespoon vegetable shortening. Microwave on high, stirring every 20 seconds, until melted and smooth, about 1 minute, 30 seconds. Dip balls in coating, sprinkle with sprinkles, and serve at room temperature. Repeat with remaining candy melts and shortening until all balls are coated. (If coating becomes too solid to use, simply microwave it until melted again, stirring every 20 seconds.)

Sweet 'n' Spicy MIXED NUTS

THESE CANDIED NUTS HAVE A TOUCH OF SPICE in them that will delight your taste buds. A perfect addition to a cheese plate, they're also great on ice cream or simply by the handful. Try them with pecans, cashews, or your favorite mixed nut blend.

1 LARGE EGG WHITE

3/4 TEASPOON VANILLA EXTRACT

1 TEASPOON SHERRY (OR COOKING SHERRY)

1/2 CUP SUGAR

1 TEASPOON GROUND CINNAMON

1/2 TEASPOON GROUND NUTMEG

1/8 TEASPOON CAYENNE PEPPER

1/2 TEASPOON KOSHER SALT

1 (16-OUNCE) PACKAGE MIXED NUTS

1. In medium bowl, combine egg white, vanilla, and sherry. In separate medium bowl, combine sugar, cinnamon, nutmeg, pepper, and salt. Add pecan halves to bowl of wet ingredients and stir to combine, then add to dry ingredients and stir until pecans are coated.

2. Line air fryer basket with parchment paper and set to 250º. Working in batches, place nuts in a single layer. Cook until toasted, about 30 minutes, shaking or stirring once during cooking time. Repeat with remaining nuts.

Five Spice SHORTBREAD

THIS SHORTBREAD RECIPE IS BUTTERY, crisp-yet-tender, and simply melts in your mouth. I love dipping them in this five spice mixture, which has hints of Christmastime, but they're just as delicious plain!

---

6 TABLESPOONS (3/4 STICK) UNSALTED BUTTER, SOFTENED

1/3 CUP SUGAR

1/2 TEASPOON KOSHER SALT

1 EGG YOLK

1 TABLESPOON VANILLA EXTRACT

1 1/4 CUP ALL-PURPOSE FLOUR

2 TABLESPOONS FIVE SPICE POWDER

1/4 CUP TURBINADO OR OTHER GRANULATED SUGAR

COOKING SPRAY

1. In the bowl of a mixer or a large bowl, combine the butter, sugar, and salt and blend on medium speed (or vigorously whisk) until creamed, about 2 minutes. Add the egg yolk and mix until incorporated. Then add the vanilla extract.

2. If using a mixer, turn it off and add the flour, then turn the machine back on to low. If mixing by hand, add flour little by little while continuing to whisk. Remove the dough from the bowl. Working on parchment or wax paper, form the dough into a logs that are about 10 inches long and 1¼ inches in diameter. Wrap in the paper and place in the freezer overnight or until ready to use.

3. In a small bowl, combine five spice powder and sugar.

4. Cut chilled log into twenty 12-inch rounds. Spray each round on all sides with cooking spray, then dip one cut surface of each round into the spice mixture.

5. Set the air fryer to 350ºF. Working in batches, place cookies spice mixture–side up, in a single layer in the air fryer basket, leaving space between each one. Cook until golden brown, about 10 to 12 minutes. Remove the cookies with a spatula and cool on a wire rack. Repeat with remaining cookies.

Berry COBBLER

THE SECRET TO A GOOD COBBLER is a crispy top, and the air fryer is a great tool to get it. Use fresh berries in the summer, and head to the frozen section in winter—either work great!

---

1 CUP MIXED BERRIES, FRESH OR FROZEN (THAWED)

1/4 CUP SUGAR

4 TABLESPOONS ALL-PURPOSE FLOUR, DIVIDED

1 TEASPOON LEMON ZEST

2 TABLESPOONS SOFTENED BUTTER

2 TABLESPOONS PACKED BROWN SUGAR

1 TABLESPOON INSTANT OATMEAL

1/4 TEASPOON VANILLA EXTRACT

1. In an over-safe bowl that fits in your air fryer, combine berries, sugar, 2 tablespoons flour, and lemon zest; set aside.

2. In a mixing bowl, use a fork to mix together remaining 2 tablespoons flour, butter, brown sugar, instant oatmeal, and vanilla.

The mixture should be crumbly in consistency. Place crumble on top of berry mixture.

3. Set air fryer to 325°F. Place baking dish in the air fryer basket, and cook until berries are bubbly and topping is browned, 15 to 20 minutes.

Dessert EGG ROLLS
with Chocolate Dipping Sauce

THESE DESSERT EGG ROLLS ARE A TAKE ON FRIED BANANAS, a classic Thai dessert. They're a great way to get your family to eat fruit, but they're equally impressive at a party.

---

2 LARGE BANANAS

1/4 CUP MINI MARSHMALLOWS

10 EGG ROLL WRAPPERS

COOKING SPRAY

1/2 CUP HEAVY CREAM

3/4 CUP DARK CHOCOLATE CHIPS

POWDERED SUGAR, FOR DUSTING

1. Cut banana into 10 equal pieces. Roll out egg roll wrapper and place banana and several mini marshmallows in center. Brush outer edges with water and roll in ends on top of filling.

2. Set air fryer to 400ºF. Working in batches, spray dessert egg rolls on all sides and place in single layer in air fryer basket. Cook for 10 minutes, turning halfway through cooking time.

3. In the meantime, make chocolate dipping sauce: In a medium bowl, combine cream and chocolate chips. Heat on medium-high (70%) power for 40 seconds, then stir. Continue to heat in 20-second increments, stirring each time, until it's fully combined.

4. Dust dessert egg rolls with powdered sugar and serve with warm dipping sauce.

INDEXES

CHRONOLOGICAL LIST OF RECIPES ———

ALPHABETICAL LIST OF RECIPES

METRIC CONVERSIONS

VOLUME

US	METRIC
1/8 TEASPOON	.5 MILLILITERS
1/4 TEASPOON	1 MILLILITERS
1/2 TEASPOON	2 MILLILITERS
3/4 TEASPOON	4 MILLILITERS
1 TEASPOON	5 MILLILITERS
1 TABLESPOON	15 MILLILITERS
1/4 CUP	60 MILLILITERS
1/3 CUP	80 MILLILITERS
1/2 CUP	120 MILLILITERS
2/3 CUP	160 MILLILITERS
3/4 CUP	180 MILLILITERS
1 CUP	225 MILLILITERS (DRY), 250 MILLILITERS (LIQUID)
2 CUPS (1 PINT)	450 MILLILITERS, 500 MILLILITERS (LIQUID)
4 CUPS (1 QUART)	1 LITER
1/2 GALLON	2 LITERS
1 GALLON	4 LITERS

WEIGHT

US	METRIC
1 OUNCE	28 GRAMS
4 OUNCES (1/4 POUND)	113 GRAMS
8 OUNCES (1/2 POUND)	230 GRAMS
12 OUNCES (3/4 POUND)	340 GRAMS
16 OUNCES (1 POUND)	450 GRAMS
23 OUNCES (2 POUNDS)	900 GRAMS

LENGTH

US	METRIC
1/4 INCH	6 MILLIMETERS
1/2 INCH	13 MILLIMETERS
3/4 INCH	19 MILLIMETERS
1 INCH	2 1/2 CENTIMETERS
1 1/2 INCHES	3 3/4 CENTIMETERS
2 INCHES	5 CENTIMETERS
2 1/2 INCHES	6 1/2 CENTIMETERS

AIR FRYER TEMPERATURES

FAHRENHEIT	CELSIUS
250°F	120°C
275°F	140°C
300°F	150°C
325°F	170°C
350°F	180°C
375°F	190°C
400°F	200°C
425°F	220°C
450°F	230°C
475°F	240°C
500°F	260°C